Past Praise for the KNOWING JESUS SERIES

"In true Tara-Leigh fashion, this study is easy to follow while also challenging you to dig deeper into what the Word is saying. It's more than simply reading the Bible and answering some questions. It's a test to gauge your spiritual walk, to ask the hard questions, and to be challenged with each turn of the page about what the Holy Spirit is revealing. Whether you are a new believer or well-versed in theological teachings, this study has something to offer everyone."

Clare Thompson Sims, D-Group member

"This study delivers what D-Group has been doing for years. Instead of feeding the readers answers, it empowers them to do the work of arriving at answers through the careful study and close reading of God's Word, allowing them to take ownership of their continued growth and faith in King Jesus. What a thrilling start of a memorable new series!"

Zuzana Johansen, D-Group member

"This study helps the reader connect the Old Testament with the New by giving the perspective of the Jewish culture and customs during Jesus's day. This lens provides clarity as to why Jesus ministered and spoke as He did while interacting with both Jews and Gentiles. It also clearly communicates the relevance and life-changing power of Jesus's teachings for Christians today. It's a road map, pulling from the pages of the Old Testament and connecting it to the Gospels, pointing to our victory in Christ on the cross."

Jeremy Hall, D-Group member

"*Knowing Jesus as King* combines a deep dive into the book of Matthew with the structure of D-Group. Having been in D-Group from the very start—fifteen years ago—I can confidently say the structure creates the consistency it demands and bears much fruit for any believer. Buckle up and have faith that God will reveal Himself to you as the promised and present King over the next ten weeks."

Meghann Glenn, D-Group charter member

KNOWING
JESUS
AS GOD

Also by Tara-Leigh Cobble

The Bible Recap:
A One-Year Guide to Reading and Understanding the Entire Bible

The Bible Recap Study Guide:
Daily Questions to Deepen Your Understanding of the Entire Bible

The Bible Recap Journal:
Your Daily Companion to the Entire Bible

The Bible Recap Discussion Guide:
Weekly Questions for Group Conversation on the Entire Bible

The Bible Recap Kids' Devotional:
365 Reflections and Activities for Children and Families

The God Shot:
100 Snapshots of God's Character in Scripture

Israel:
Beauty, Light, and Luxury

The Bible Recap for Kids:
A 365-Day Guide through the Bible for Young Readers

THE BIBLE RECAP KNOWING JESUS SERIES*

Knowing Jesus as King:
A 10-Session Study on the Gospel of Matthew

Knowing Jesus as Servant:
A 10-Session Study on the Gospel of Mark

Knowing Jesus as Savior:
A 10-Session Study on the Gospel of Luke

Knowing Jesus as God:
A 10-Session Study on the Gospel of John

*General editor

THE *BIBLE RECAP* KNOWING JESUS SERIES

KNOWING JESUS AS GOD

A 10-SESSION STUDY ON THE GOSPEL OF JOHN

TARA-LEIGH COBBLE,
GENERAL EDITOR

WRITTEN BY THE D-GROUP THEOLOGY & CURRICULUM TEAM

BETHANYHOUSE
a division of Baker Publishing Group
Minneapolis, Minnesota

© 2024 by Tara-Leigh Cobble

Published by Bethany House Publishers
Minneapolis, Minnesota
BethanyHouse.com

Bethany House Publishers is a division of
Baker Publishing Group, Grand Rapids, Michigan

Printed in the United States of America

ISBN 9780764243592 (paper)
ISBN 9781493446902 (ebook)

Library of Congress Cataloging-in-Publication Control Number: 2024031712

Unless otherwise indicated, Scripture quotations are from The Holy Bible, English Standard Version® (ESV®), copyright © 2001 by Crossway, a publishing ministry of Good News Publishers. Used by permission. All rights reserved. ESV Text Edition: 2016

Scripture quotations identified KJV are from the King James Version of the Bible.

Scripture quotations identified NLT are taken from the *Holy Bible*, New Living Translation, copyright © 1996, 2004, 2015 by Tyndale House Foundation. Used by permission of Tyndale House Publishers, Carol Stream, Illinois 60188. All rights reserved.

The D-Group Theology & Curriculum Team is Meredith Knox, Liz Suggs, Meg Mitchell, Laura Buchelt, Emily Pickell, Tara-Leigh Cobble.

The general editor is represented by Alive Literary Agency, www.AliveLiterary.com.

Interior design by Nadine Rewa
Cover design by Dan Pitts
Author image from © Meshali Mitchell

Baker Publishing Group publications use paper produced from sustainable forestry practices and postconsumer waste whenever possible.

24 25 26 27 28 29 30   7 6 5 4 3 2 1

CONTENTS

INTRODUCTION

The gospel of John is often recommended to new believers because it paints a clear picture of the deity of Jesus. John's writing style has a reputation for being shallow enough for a child to wade in, while also being deep enough for an elephant to freely swim. The message is clear, but the words contain a depth you could study every day for the rest of your life and still learn something new on your deathbed.

Like the authors of the other three gospels, John doesn't introduce himself explicitly. It's generally accepted within Christian tradition that the author is "the disciple Jesus loved." John was called to be a disciple along with his brother James (Mark 1:19–20). These brothers, the sons of Zebedee, were fishermen by trade, yet they became two of the three disciples Jesus kept closest to Himself throughout His ministry. James was the first of the disciples to be killed for his faith (Acts 12:2), while John is believed to have been the last of the twelve to die. John is also credited with penning a trio of New Testament letters (1–3 John) and the book of Revelation.

Though John isn't clear about who he's writing his gospel account for, we know it was written after the other three gospels, and it provided information the others left out. It's generally accepted that John wrote his gospel late in his life, probably around AD 85–95. In 20:31, John tells us his motivation for writing: "These are written so that you may believe that Jesus is the Christ, the Son of God, and that by believing you may have life in his name."

To accomplish his purpose of showing readers that Jesus is God the Son, John tells his readers about Jesus's seven public signs, or miracles, as well as seven different times Jesus used metaphorical *I am* statements.

(In Judaism and Scripture, the number seven symbolizes fulfillment and completion!) Each of the signs shows readers the heavenly authority Jesus had on earth, while the seven metaphorical *I am* statements point readers back to Exodus 3:14, where God told Moses His name: "I AM WHO I AM." This sacred and holy name referred exclusively to God, and Jesus claimed it for Himself *seven* times. Be on the lookout for the *I am*'s and public signs of Jesus:

Seven Metaphorical *I Am*'s

"I am the bread of life"—6:48
"I am the light of the world"—8:12
"I am the door"—10:9
"I am the good shepherd"—10:11
"I am the resurrection and the life"—11:25
"I am the way, the truth, and the life"—14:6
"I am the vine"—15:5

Seven Public Signs (Miracles)

Water into wine—2:2–11
Healing a nobleman's son—4:46–54
Healing a man at Bethesda—5:2–9
Feeding five thousand—6:1–14
Walking on the Sea of Galilee—6:16–21
Healing the blind man—9:1–7
Raising Lazarus from the dead—11:1–44

As we study, we'll find strong arguments against the idea that Jesus never claimed deity, we'll see Jesus buck against man-made tradition, and we'll watch Him embody His full humanity alongside His full divinity. Whether it's your first time studying John or your hundredth, the simplicity and complexity of this gospel account make it compelling to dig into together. So let's get started!

HOW TO USE THIS STUDY

While Bible study is vital to the Christian walk, a well-rounded spiritual life comes from engaging with other spiritual disciplines as well. This study is designed not only to equip you with greater knowledge and theological depth, but to help you engage in other formative practices that will create a fuller, more fulfilling relationship with Jesus. We want to see you thrive in every area of your life with God!

Content and Questions

In each of the ten weeks of this study, the teaching and questions are divided into six days, but feel free to do it all at once if that's more manageable for your schedule. If you choose to complete each week's study in one sitting (especially if that time occurs later in the study-week), keep in mind that there are aspects you will want to be mindful of each day: the daily Bible reading, Scripture memorization, and the weekly challenge. Those are best attended to throughout the week.

Daily Bible Reading

The daily Bible reading corresponds to our study. It will take an average of three minutes per day to simply read (not study) the text. If you're an auditory learner, you may prefer to listen to an audio version of these Bible chapters.

Even if you decide to do the week's content and questions in one sitting, we still encourage you to make the daily Bible reading a part of your regular daily rhythm. Establishing a habit of reading the Word every day will help fortify your faith and create greater connections with God.

If you decide to break the study up into the six allotted days each week, your daily Bible reading will align with your study. Days 1–5 will follow our study of John, Day 6 features a psalm that corresponds to our reading, and Day 7 serves as a catch-up day in case you fall behind.

Scripture Memorization

Memorizing Scripture isn't busywork! It's an important part of hiding God's Word in our hearts (Psalm 119:11). Our memorization passage—John 15:1–11—focuses on our unity with God. We encourage you to practice it cumulatively—that is, *add* to what you're practicing each week instead of *replacing* it. We quote the English Standard Version (and some of our resources are in that translation as well), but feel free to memorize it in whatever translation you prefer. We suggest working on each week's verse(s) throughout the week, not just at the last minute. We've provided some free tools to help you with this, including a weekly verse song: MyDGroup.org/Resources/John.

Weekly Challenge

This is our practical response to what we've learned each week. We want to be "doers of the word, and not hearers only" (James 1:22). You'll find a variety of challenges, and we encourage you to lean into them all—especially the ones you find *most* challenging! This will help strengthen your spiritual muscles and encourage you in your faith. As with the memory verse, you'll want to begin this practice earlier in the week, especially because some weekly challenges include things to do each day of the week (e.g., prayers, journaling, etc.).

Resources

This is a Scripture-heavy study, and you'll find yourself looking up passages often. If you're new to studying Scripture, this will be a great way to dig in and sharpen your skills! You will feel more equipped and less intimidated as you move through each chapter. Some questions may ask you to refer to a Bible dictionary, commentary, or Greek or Hebrew lexi-con, but you don't need to purchase those tools. There are lots of free options available online. We've linked to some of our favorite tools—plus additional resources such as podcasts, articles, and apps—at MyDGroup .org/Resources/John.

Groups

Because each week has a lot of questions in the content, we offer the follow-ing recommendation for those who plan to discuss the study in a weekly group meeting. As each member is doing their homework, we suggest they mark their favorite items with a star and mark any confusing items with a question mark. This serves as preparation for the group discussion and helps direct the conversation in beneficial ways.

John 1–3:
The Word of God

Note: If you haven't yet read How to Use This Study on pages 11–13, please do that before continuing. It will provide you with a proper framework and helpful tools.

DAILY BIBLE READING

Day 1: John 1:1–28
Day 2: John 1:29–51
Day 3: John 2:1–25
Day 4: John 3:1–21
Day 5: John 3:22–36
Day 6: Psalm 19
Day 7: Catch-Up Day

Corresponds to Days 274 and 279 of *The Bible Recap.*

WEEKLY CHALLENGE

See page 37 for more information.

John 1:1–28

 READ JOHN 1:1-28

1. **Review 1:1–5 and compare it to Genesis 1:1–5.** What similarities do you see?

Every generation tends to get stuck in its ways—from cultural biases to social media feeds. Using Genesis 1:1–5 as his outline, John helped us all step outside of ourselves and into the greater story, the one God has been writing since "the beginning."

2. **Count how many times John used the word** *word* **in 1:1.** Why do you think this is important?

In Greek, this is the word *logos*. John's use of this word would've connected with both Jews and Greeks who used it in their everyday lives. In conversations among Jewish rabbis, the *logos*—Word of God—could be used to refer to God Himself. In ancient Greek philosophy, *logos* was the "ultimate reason" that controlled all things, bringing order and meaning to life's chaos. These two groups had different approaches to making sense of the world, but the questions that plagued them remained the same:

> *What is the way to wisdom?*
> *What is the source of all truth?*
> *What is the real meaning of life?*

Though we may not be throwing *logos* around as often as rabbis in the temple or Greek Gnostics over glasses of wine, aren't we asking the same questions today? Reaching back to the very foundations of the world, John grabbed the genesis of creation and pulled it into the present to reveal a truth that affects all humans across all time:

> Jesus was with God, and Jesus is God.

3. **Review 1:6–18.**

In 1:12–13, John revealed another emphasis of his gospel: belief. You'll see this theme repeatedly. Jesus is God, indeed—but for us to *receive* His salvation, we must *believe* He is who He says He is.

4. John's gospel introduces us to another man named John in today's passage. **Read the following verses, then circle which John the text referred to.** (For clarity, we will lovingly refer to John the Baptist by the initials JTB.)

1:6	JTB	John the apostle
1:15	JTB	John the apostle
1:19	JTB	John the apostle
1:26	JTB	John the apostle
1:28	JTB	John the apostle

There were about as many Johns walking around ancient Israel as there were Marys, so it's helpful for us to take notice of which John is doing and saying what. John the apostle never referred to himself by name in his gospel but rather as "the disciple whom Jesus loved." JTB did not write the gospel of John; John "the beloved apostle" did.

5. In 1:14, we see the revelation of "God with us." Write the verse below, then circle the portion that means the most to you.

This verse could be literally translated as "the Word became flesh and *tabernacled* among us." Surely when the original audience heard this, they felt their breath catch in their chests. The tabernacle was the epicenter of Jewish life in the Old Testament. It was the very dwelling place of God. The most holy of holy places. Every tent of dwelling was pointed toward the tabernacle, signifying the presence of God as the focus of all life, both personal and communal.

Here, John implied that this holy epicenter—this place of hope and power—was no longer a place at all. Instead, the tabernacle was walking around in flesh and blood, granting access and presence to any and all who would believe in Him.

This was earth-shattering news for people who had waited centuries for a mere glimpse of glory. In one man, all were welcome. God could be known, and He could be known personally and intimately—in Jesus.

6. Pause for a moment and thank Jesus for being available to you anytime, anywhere. If you've never felt God's presence with you (or if it has been a while), ask Jesus to reveal Himself to you now. Through the presence of the Holy Spirit, He *still* dwells with us.

7. Review 1:19–28, then read Isaiah 40:3.

JTB's testimony was not a story about himself. It was about Jesus. What he did and said pointed to Christ. JTB's mission had been clear since before he was born: "Make straight the way of the Lord."

8. Our testimonies should point beyond us to the work and person of Jesus. Consider your own story now. How have you (intentionally or accidentally) made your testimony about yourself? How can you use it to point to Jesus instead?

John 1:29–51

 READ JOHN 1:29–51

1. Review 1:29–34.

To behold means "to be sure to see." Today is about slowing down and heeding JTB's call to see Jesus for who He truly is. We'll examine six encounters and how each individual beheld Jesus. May God give us eyes to see Him rightly.

2. In 1:29, John revealed Jesus as the Lamb of God. Match the Old Testament passages to Jesus's fulfillment of them as the perfect sacrifice.

Genesis 3:21	Jesus is the lamb God would provide for Himself as a substitute for Isaac.
Genesis 22:8–14	Jesus is the animal slain in the garden to cover the sin and shame of Adam and Eve.
Exodus 12:21–24	Jesus is the silent and prophesied lamb being led to the slaughter.
Leviticus 4:32–35	Jesus is the lamb sacrificed as a guilt offering according to Levitical law.
Isaiah 53:7	Jesus is the Passover lamb provided to save Israel from death.

John is the only New Testament writer who referred to Jesus as the Lamb of God. Later, when he wrote the book of Revelation, he used this name twenty-seven times. Revelation 13:8 says that Jesus was the Lamb who was slain "before the foundation of the world." Once again, John was pointing us back to the beginning. The cross of Christ was the eternal plan.

In 1:32–34, the presence of the Spirit and the voice of the Father confirmed Jesus's union in this plan. At His baptism, the presence of the Spirit hovered over Jesus just as He did over the waters in Genesis 1:2. The voice of the Father affirmed His identity as "Son of God." We can be saved *only* by the sacrifice of Jesus Christ and by believing in His divine Sonship.

3. Review 1:35–42.

4. Fill in the blanks with John's first recorded words of Jesus.

"What are you _____?"

"_____, and you will _____."

Before you review the remaining disciples' responses, notice that these are the prompts that preceded them. Encountering Jesus requires that we wrestle with this same question and invitation. The revelation of Jesus's identity comes with a confronting reality: Either we take Him seriously and follow Him, or we do not. Neutrality is not an option.

5. Review 1:43–51.

6. Match the disciple with their response to Jesus.

Andrew	Announces Jesus as the Son of God and king of Israel
Simon Peter	Reveals Jesus as the fulfillment of the law and prophets
Philip	Receives a new identity
Nathanael	Pronounces Jesus as the Messiah

Fun fact: The unnamed disciple mentioned in 1:37 and 1:40 is believed to be the author John himself. We'll count him in our six total encounters of the day. But more important than the disciples' identities were the revelations they had about *Jesus's* identity. In just the first chapter of John's gospel, he gave us a kaleidoscope of theological colors through which to see Jesus: the Word, the creator, the life, the light of men, the new tabernacle, grace and truth, the revelation of God, the Lamb of God, the Messiah, the transformer of identities, the fulfillment of the Old Testament law and prophets, the Son of God, and the king of Israel.

John was determined for us to see Jesus as our one true Messiah, or "anointed one." Jesus was the one set apart from the beginning of time to take away the sins of the world. Every prophecy pointed to Him. Every sacrifice was fulfilled in Him. Every word of the law was spoken to reveal Him as the living Word. This Jesus, He is God. Take notice.

And if that wasn't enough, John had one more color to add to our Messiah mosaic.

7. Read 1:51 and Genesis 28:12. What else was John revealing about Jesus's identity? If you need help, use your favorite Bible commentary.

8. End the day by looking at all the titles of Jesus listed in the first paragraph on this page. Circle the one that is most impactful to you right now. Below, write a prayer of gratitude for who Jesus is and how He has revealed Himself to you.

John 2:1–25

 READ JOHN 2:1–25

Today, we're introduced to the first of seven public signs Jesus performs in John's gospel. Think of these signs as signage. On modern highways, the signs point to and reveal the destination. Likewise, Jesus's signs were never solely about the signs themselves but about what they pointed to and signified about Jesus—His identity, His mission, His heart.

1. **Review 2:1–12.**

Take special notice of the interaction between Jesus and His mother in 2:1–5. We don't have a great English word for it, but in the original language, *woman* was a term of endearment or respect. Modern translations of this encounter may seem shocking or confusing, but rest assured: Jesus loved His mama.

As this wedding party picked up, the wine ran out. For many modern readers, that would simply mean it was time to switch to sparkling water or Coke Zero. But in ancient Israel, a wedding running out of wine was a great public shame. Mary brought this to Jesus's attention, and He responded with a refrain we often see in the Gospels, "My hour has not yet come." These six words revealed a massive reality in which Jesus, the Father, and the Spirit were always in alliance. Because Jesus is God, He always operated in perfect unity with the Godhead throughout His ministry, and the Trinity always had a divinely timed plan in place. We'll continue to see that plan unfold in perfect order.

Mary revered Jesus by telling the servants to do what He said. She wasn't disrespecting His timing but honoring His power. She knew what He was capable of.

2. When we read familiar stories, it can be easy to skim. But if we miss the rich details, we miss the beauty. Using 2:6–10 as your guide, fill in the table below.

How many stone water jars were available?	
What were the jars usually used for?	
How many gallons could each jar hold?	
What was the servants' response to Jesus's direction?	
What was the master of the feast's response upon tasting the new wine?	
Did the master know where the new wine came from?	

You may recall a miracle performed in Exodus 7:14–25, where Moses and Aaron turned the water of the Nile into blood. With that first plague, God revealed Himself as a greater source than the Nile (and its goddess Hapi) the Egyptians had come to trust. It was the first step to the Israelites' freedom.

With this sign at the wedding—the first of His seven signs in this gospel—Jesus was signifying Himself as the *better* Moses. Moses turned water to blood, but Jesus turned water to *wine*. But the wine was just the sign; it wasn't the point. Jesus was—and still is—the point of this sign.

In ancient Israel, diluted wine was a drink more common than water (as water was difficult to keep clean). By turning the water into wine, Jesus revealed Himself as a greater source than both wine *and* water. He is the ultimate source we should rely on for survival, community, and joyous celebration. The fact that this miracle was housed in jars normally reserved for purification revealed Him as the one who was the new way to true purity from sin.

Jesus was doing far more than just keeping the party going.

3. **Review 2:13–22.**

This is the first of three Passovers mentioned in John (though his order may not be chronological). Given that Passover involved massive crowds, it's almost certain that this scene took place in front of many witnesses.

4. How did Jesus's public anger make you feel?

5. What was the significance of Him pausing to make a whip?

The problem at the temple was not the money changers; people had to pay the traditional temple tax. The problem was not the trade of animals; people needed to purchase animals for sacrifice after a long journey to Jerusalem. The problem was *how* and *where* business was being conducted.

There were tens of thousands of Jews visiting Jerusalem for the Passover, and salesmen seized the opportunity. With so much need for sacrifice, why not pocket a few extra coins? It is believed that they would mark up the sales of animals, even buying "unclean" sacrifices from pilgrims and reselling them at a profit to the next needy traveler, price-gouging and taking advantage of the tourists.

What's more, they probably set up in the court of the Gentiles. This was the only place non-Jews were allowed to worship. The Gentiles would've felt even more out of place among the crowd of merchant tables and money lenders. As John revealed in 1:29, Jesus came to take away the sins of the world—people from among *every nation*. Engaging in these practices made it more difficult and expensive for people to enter His presence—and that was grounds for intentional and confrontational cleansing. Jesus made room, and Jesus made it pure. Any space intended for people to encounter His presence should do the same.

In 2:18–22, Jesus revealed Himself as the new temple. Through His death and resurrection—which we'll cover in the final section of this study—He made the presence of God available to everyone, everywhere. The way He carried this information is known as the messianic secret—which is just a way of saying He was intentional with the timing of revealing His identity as Messiah.

6. Review 2:23–25. Our day ends with Jesus's knowledge of "what was in man." Using Psalm 51:10–12 as a prayer guide, ask the Holy Spirit if there is any space where He needs to confront and cleanse what is inside you.

John 3:1–21

 READ JOHN 3:1–21

1. Review 3:1–2, and with the help of a quick web search, complete this profile of Nicodemus.

My name is Nicodemus, which means "_____."

My occupation	
My position in the Jewish community	
My favorite time to visit Jesus	

Nicodemus already had some insight into who Jesus was. But unlike many other Pharisees, he had not written Jesus off.

2. Review 3:1–15.

It was common practice for rabbis to engage in question-and-answer dialogue to seek wisdom and deepen understanding. It served as a sign of respect and honor. Nicodemus's rare vulnerability and honest curiosity drove him to seek Jesus out for himself. Jesus responded with honor by engaging in a lengthy conversation with him.

3. What three questions did Nicodemus ask Jesus? Write them below.

Jesus and Nicodemus began their rabbinical exchange with a conversation about being "born again." According to Jewish teaching, Israelites were reserved a place in heaven simply because they were descendants of Abraham. But Jesus was clear: A pedigree does not ensure access to eternal life. We must be born *again*—to a new family and a new life.

4. Read Ezekiel 36:25–28 and revisit John 1:12–13. How did John reveal that Jesus was the fulfillment of this Old Testament prophecy?

John was consistent with the message that we aren't made "right" by any outward accomplishment or biological bloodline. Salvation is not hereditary. It may feel better to hold up good works and family trees as "proof" of our righteousness. But heavenly realities can't be accomplished by earthly pursuits. To access the family of God, the abundant life of the Spirit, and the eternal hope of heaven, we must take our minds off earthly things and set them on heavenly things. Jesus is the prophetic fulfillment of being washed "from all your uncleannesses." He is the only one who can ensure a new heart. He is the guarantee of a new spirit.

5. In 3:13–14, Jesus clarified His authority to make such claims. Using a commentary, look up the significance of the title Son of Man. Then read Numbers 21:4–9. What do you think John is revealing about Jesus's identity?

Nicodemus would have been very familiar with this story, but it was highly unlikely that he understood its full meaning at that moment. Keep this story in mind when we meet him again in John 19. Could it be that this quiet conversation came roaring back to him as he beheld Jesus hanging on the cross?

6. **Review 3:16–21.**

7. You may have heard 3:16 since infancy, but it's important to read this verse with the entire thought presented in 3:17–19. As a tool to help you study the text and not just observe it, circle the correct answers based on the text below.

What was God's motivation for sending Jesus?	Love	Wrath
What was Jesus's main mission?	Condemnation	Salvation
What does one receive when they believe in Jesus?	Eternal life	A better life
What does one receive when they do not believe in Jesus?	Judgment	A second chance

How incredible is it that this famous passage was quoted to the man who seemed to need it the least? Sometimes those of us who are most familiar with the Bible need the greatest reminders of the beautiful and powerful truth of the gospel.

8. **Review 3:19–21, then read 1 John 4:13–18 (John wrote that one too).** What do you think John was trying to reveal to us about light and love?

One tragic problem of our sinful nature is that it feels safer to keep things hidden. We shudder at the idea of our thoughts advertised in Times Square. *No, thank you.* It feels safer to keep parts of ourselves hidden. If we're honest, we may keep much of our life in the dark—where few (if any) are ever allowed to see. We love the dark.

When Jesus came into the world, He came for exposure. He came after the darkest parts of our lives—the sin we'd rather not see, the unhealthy patterns we'd like to keep protected. In love, He lights up the darkest parts of our hearts to reveal our great need for Him. Light does not come into a space to make peace with the dark. It comes to take over.

At first, our response may be to take offense, in the same way we immediately close our eyes when someone turns on the overhead lights in a dark room. But the only way to fall out of love with the dark and its charade of safety is to fall more in love with the Light of life Himself.

9. What is one thing you're keeping in the dark? Write out a prayer asking the Holy Spirit to give you strength to humbly expose your sin to the light of Jesus's love.

John 3:22–36

 READ JOHN 3:22–36

We started the week reading JTB's testimony, so why not end with another one?

Side note: It may not seem like much, but John's parenthetical explanation in 3:24 is an example of a stylistic choice common in his writing that you should look for throughout the book. John added personal commentaries throughout to address questions that may have arisen among Christian communities as the other gospels circulated. It's just a fun little treasure hunt for the rest of your study.

1. Review 3:22–26, then reflect on these questions:

What was the significance of the debate over purification?

Why were JTB's disciples so upset?

These opening verses reveal two human tendencies: competition and comparison. Can you relate? We don't know exactly what the debate about purification was—maybe some Jews didn't like how JTB was practicing purification rituals by a "baptism of repentance." Apparently, it wasn't the details of the debate that were important, but rather, what it led to: JTB's disciples fearing Jesus's growing influence. It seems they wondered, *If Jesus starts to draw a crowd, what does that mean for us?*

2. Review 3:27–30, where JTB explained why this was actually a good thing. Let's rejoice with him! Using the text and some Bible study tools, complete the following table.

Fill in the blanks	"A person _____ receive even _____ _____ unless it is _____ him from _____."
Fill in the blanks	"I am _____ _____ _____ . . ."
What is a "bridegroom"?	
What was JTB's relationship with the bridegroom?	
What was JTB's response to his role?	
Fill in the blanks	"He must _____, but I must _____."

Six times, and in six different ways, JTB said Jesus's growing following was the entire point. Not only was JTB intent that Jesus surpass him in both followers and fame, but it completed his joy!

3. Look up Isaiah 62:3–5.

The apostle John and JTB were working together to reveal something beautiful about the bridegroom.

First, Jesus's divinity was being revealed. The Old Testament referred to God as the "bridegroom" of Israel. Jesus was the bridegroom sent for His global bride. In other words, *Jesus is God.*

Second, the whole point of a wedding was the bride and the bridegroom. If you're ever in a wedding party, you know you're there in a supporting role only. In Jewish wedding tradition, the "friend of the bridegroom" handled many of the wedding details and even brought the bride to the bridegroom—and then, he faded into the background. JTB was telling his disciples, "I am doing my job. The bride of the future church is going toward the bridegroom. And nothing could make me happier."

JTB ended by speaking of the "increase" of Jesus. We know Jesus is already perfect; so for Jesus to "increase" didn't mean that He could get bigger or better somehow. JTB was implying that his own decrease magnified Jesus's inherent greatness to the world around him.

The Godhead (Father, Son, and Spirit) has always been doing this—magnifying one another and giving glory to one another. Knowing he was made in their image, JTB followed suit. He was obsessed with the person of Jesus, pointing from himself to pour more glory on Christ.

4. Review 3:31–36. JTB concluded by magnifying the person of Jesus. Circle the point of magnification that is most impactful or that is new to you.

Jesus was sent from above and is above all.

Jesus had seen and heard from the Father Himself.

Jesus spoke the very words of God.

Jesus was full of the Holy Spirit.

Jesus was able to give the Spirit "without measure."

Jesus was fully loved by the Father.

Jesus was entrusted with everything that belonged to God.

JTB knew true joy was found in magnifying the life of Christ. And his joyous magnification of Jesus always ended with an invitation: Believe in Him and live, or disobey and remain judged. This was kindness to call everyone to belief and repentance (Romans 2:4). It is still kindness today.

May our lives also be complete as we join JTB and magnify Christ together! He's where the joy is!

5. What stood out to you most in this week's study? Why?

6. What did you learn or relearn about God and His character this week?

Corresponding Psalm & Prayer

 READ PSALM 19

1. What correlation do you see between Psalm 19 and this week's study of Jesus as God?

2. What portions of this psalm stand out to you most?

3. Close by praying this prayer aloud:

Father,

  Even the skies can't stop themselves from praising You! Their endless beauty proclaims Your endless glory. Your Son is the Word: the fulfillment of the goodness, truth, and beauty of Scripture. The

Most Holy One came down to live among us and to redeem us. You are worthy of all our worship and all our praise.

Yet even though John the Baptist taught us how to magnify Your Son, most of my thoughts are more concerned with my temporary troubles than Your eternal goodness. And even though John the disciple implored us to believe, I don't always live like I do.

Like David wrote in the psalm, Your law is perfect and makes simple people like me wise. Lord, make me wise. May my prayer and study—the words of my mouth and the meditation of my heart—be acceptable in Your sight. May they be the winds that carry me closer to You all the days of my life. And may I realize that I'm not carrying myself, but that You are carrying me.

Like His disciples, may I follow Jesus all the days of my life.

I surrender my life to You, Lord—every moment of my day, each decision I make, I yield my will and way to Your perfect will and way.

I love You too. Amen.

Rest, Catch Up, or Dig Deeper

 WEEKLY CHALLENGE

Days 1 and 5 reveal that JTB's testimony was all about Jesus. He never made it about himself. This week, take a moment to write your testimony and evaluate whether it points more to you or to Jesus. After you've taken stock (and perhaps done some editing), share your testimony about Jesus with a friend.

Scripture to Memorize

Every branch in me that
does not bear fruit he takes
away, and every branch that
does bear fruit he prunes,
that it may bear more fruit.

John 15:2

John 4–5
The Authority of God

DAILY BIBLE READING

Day 1: John 4:1–30

Day 2: John 4:31–54

Day 3: John 5:1–17

Day 4: John 5:18–29

Day 5: John 5:30–47

Day 6: Psalm 36

Day 7: Catch-Up Day

Corresponds to Days 279 and 281 of *The Bible Recap*.

WEEKLY CHALLENGE

See page 61 for more information.

John 4:1–30

 READ JOHN 4:1–30

1. Review 4:1–6.

News of Jesus's ministry had spread to the Pharisees, so Jesus headed north to Galilee. Pious Jews preferred to avoid Samaria, a region they considered "unclean," so they would take the long route from the Judean wilderness to lush Galilee, but John said Jesus "had to pass through Samaria."

2. Use a Bible commentary to answer these context questions:

> What happened in Sychar (ancient Shechem) that was significant to the Jews?

> Who were the Samaritan people, and why did the Jews consider them unclean?

Jesus was fully God, but He was also a human, so it's no surprise that He grew hot and weary from the day's journey through the desert. It was customary (and practical) for women to draw water in the cooler hours of the day, so the well was probably quiet at noon as the heat began to increase.

3. Review 4:7–15.

There were two possible reasons a woman would've been at the well in the heat of the day: She had a sudden need for water, or she was a social outcast. Regardless of which reason brought her there, Jesus shattered multiple religious traditions when He spoke to this woman. Rabbis didn't speak to women in public, and especially not women from Samaria with bad reputations. But Jesus didn't just speak to her—He asked her to give Him a drink!

4. What does it reveal about the heart of God that Jesus initiated a conversation with a Samaritan woman?

Most of us haven't given much thought to the challenge of finding water, because we live with the blessing of indoor plumbing, but we would die after three days without it. In ancient Israel, drinking water came from three primary sources: cisterns, wells, and springs. Cisterns collected groundwater from rain into a large hole in the ground. It was the least desirable water source because the cistern tended to collect more than just water (use your imagination). Wells typically had clean water from an underground spring, but significant effort was required to collect that water. Springs were the preferred source of water because they were clean, fresh, and easy to draw from.

Jesus began their conversation by talking about things in the physical realm, but transitioned quickly to the spiritual realm; however, the woman didn't track with His transition.

5. If Jesus wasn't talking about physical water, what was He talking about in 4:10 and 4:13–14?

The woman's response to Jesus's offer of eternal, living water was logical and practical, because she was still thinking in the physical realm. If Jesus could make her life easier and provide more convenience, she was all in! But Jesus, speaking of the spiritual realm, knew she would have to grasp His message and confront the turmoil in her life before taking Him up on the offer.

6. Do you find yourself looking to Jesus to make your life easier and more convenient without dealing with your turmoil? Why does this mindset leave us unsatisfied?

7. Review 4:16–30.

Jesus knew every detail of the woman's situation, but He masterfully provided the opportunity for *her* to bring the truth into the light.

8. What was the woman's tumultuous situation? How might it have caused her to be an outcast?

We don't know how the woman ended up in this situation, but one interesting theory is that she was barren. When she couldn't produce children for her husbands, they divorced her, leaving her with no choice but to remarry for the sake of provision. And not only was divorce a major reason for shame in that day, but so was barrenness. Whether or not that was the case, her story was probably a sensitive subject.

In 4:19, the Samaritan woman began to recognize that there was something spiritual happening. So she adjusted to a spiritual topic: worship.

Rather than engage in the who's-worshiping-correctly debate, Jesus pointed to what was coming and invited her into it.

9. **Look up this issue of worship in a commentary.** What were the two worship locations? Why was this a controversial debate?

Don't miss what happened next. Lean in. Not only did Jesus engage with this "unclean" woman who had multiple husbands—talking with her alone, no less—but He told *this* woman in no uncertain terms that He was the long-awaited Messiah! Not just a rabbi. Not just a philosopher. Not just a righteous man. *The Messiah*. The one who would come and save people from among every tribe and nation—including hers.

Jesus's words changed this woman. She left the well where she'd been avoiding people to spread the good news in the city: The Messiah had come to them!

DAY 2

John 4:31–54

 READ JOHN 4:31–54

1. Review 4:31–38.

Just as He had with the woman at the well, Jesus gave a spiritual response to the disciples' physical suggestion that He eat. He wasn't saying they should neglect hunger, but that His primary satisfaction superseded physical needs.

2. According to Jesus, what was His primary spiritual nourishment while He was on earth?

A "four months until harvest" reference may not make much sense to us, but Jesus was referring to a common agricultural saying. There was always a gap between planting and harvesting, a natural process and timeline. Jesus wanted the disciples to view spiritual work like that; God had been at work in advance, planting the seed of the gospel, and it was time for them to reap the harvest! When God calls His followers to action to proclaim His name, we can be assured that He's already begun to work in the spaces He calls us to.

3. What are some modern examples of 4:37–38? Have you experienced anything like this—in your spiritual life or elsewhere? If so, briefly describe.

4. Review 4:39–42.

Almost immediately, Jesus's disciples got to see an example of a ripe spiritual harvest they didn't labor for. While they were talking, the woman was at work! She was telling everyone who would listen about the Man who knew everything she'd done and how He was the Messiah.

5. According to 4:39–42, which of the elements below led the people of Sychar to know that Jesus was the Savior of the world? Circle all that apply.

- The woman's testimony about Jesus

- The water from the well

- An understanding of agriculture

- Jesus's words

- The miracles Jesus performed

6. Review 4:43–45.

7. Look up 4:44 in a Bible commentary. Why was it good for Jesus to travel to a place where He was known but not honored?

8. Review 4:46–54.

Back in Cana Jesus performed His second public sign. A nobleman from Jesus's home base of Capernaum traveled about twenty miles to implore Jesus to come heal his son, who was near death. While Jesus had done miraculous signs, the signs weren't His primary objective. Jesus's response to the man may seem harsh to us, but He was addressing the broader cultural call for miracles and signs. This is evident in the original language because He used the plural form of *you* (like *you guys* or *y'all*) in His reply.

What did the man request of Jesus?	What did Jesus actually do?	Why is the difference significant?

Jesus commanded the man to go and promised that his son would live. The man chose to believe the promise and obey Jesus's command *before* he got to see the miracle. In fact, 4:51 tells us it was the servant who saw the miracle; the official saw only the result. His obedience allowed him to see the fruit of Jesus's work. Seeing the fruit deepened his belief, and as a result, his whole family believed as well. Isn't it just like Jesus to use a miracle to prove that belief in Him is more important than miracles?

Most of us would like to see the miracle before we decide to believe and obey. There is power in believing the message and truth about Jesus even when we're not seeing the miraculous. The miracles are never the point—they *point to* the point.

9. Have you ever experienced something you would describe as miraculous (no matter how wide or narrow your description of that word might be)? If so, what was your takeaway from that experience?

John 5:1–17

 READ JOHN 5:1–17

Today we see the third public sign of Jesus's ministry. Remember, it's not about the miracle itself, but about what and who the miracle points to.

1. **Review 5:1–9.**

Every year, the Jews throughout Israel packed up their families and traveled to Jerusalem for three major feasts, but John doesn't tell us which feast this was. During Passover, Pentecost, and Purim, the city of approximately twenty-five thousand would swell to approximately five times that number as people headed to the temple to meet with God.* Near the temple, there was a pool where people who were sick, injured, and disabled gathered.

2. There is probably no 5:4 in your Bible, but you may have a footnote that tells you what 5:4 says. **Use a Bible commentary to find out why this verse has been relegated to the footnotes.**

Whether 5:4 is truth or legend, the Pool of Bethesda drew in people who needed healing. One of those people was a man who had been disabled for thirty-eight years! The life expectancy for adults in first-century Israel was

---

*Scholars estimate Jerusalem's population was 25,000–55,000, and 150,000–180,000 during festivals.

around fifty-five, so whatever his age, he had probably lived most of his life in pain. And in the midst of the crowd of needy people, *Jesus saw him.*

3. What did Jesus ask the man? Why might this question seem strange?

Some say the man was there because he was satisfied with living as an invalid; after all, begging by the pool was his source of income, and the payout was likely higher during a religious feast. Others suggest he was still holding on to a sliver of hope that he would be healed.

The man assumed Jesus knew "how healing worked" at the pool, so instead of answering Jesus's question, he explained to Jesus why healing wasn't possible. It seems that, even in his wildest imagination, the man couldn't see a path forward from his disability.

4. Do you identify with either of the following? Why or why not?

A. You're comfortable managing the brokenness of your life. You'd rather continue dealing with the routine and its consequences than face the unfamiliar results of healing.

B. You want so badly to be healed from brokenness. Your whole life is consumed with the hope of gaining freedom, but you simply can't see or find the way to attain it.

Jesus responded to the man's excuse by telling him to do something the man could not physically do. In this holy moment, the man had to believe Jesus for what seemed impossible. The man didn't respond with, "But I can't, so why try?" so it's safe to assume that Jesus gave the man not only physical healing, but the very belief he needed to obey.

Seeing Jesus heal this man who had spent years in pain and need inspires hope and awe. Perhaps we even feel hopeful for healing in our own lives. But healing was only the beginning of this man's story, and it didn't end without more struggle.

5. **Use a Bible study tool to research how first-century Jews viewed the Sabbath.** What was God's original law? Which rules were man-made?

6. **Review 5:10–17.**

When John used the phrase "the Jews," it's helpful to note that he was speaking about the religious leaders who opposed Jesus, not all Jewish people.

7. How would you respond if you saw a man who had been paralyzed for thirty-eight years carrying his bed roll? How did the Jewish leaders respond? Why?

The religious leaders weren't just accusing *the man* of sinning; they were also accusing *Jesus* of sinning. They completely disregarded the fact that a miracle had taken place and only wanted to punish the "sinners," so they tried to track down the healer. But the man didn't know who Jesus was, because He had quickly slipped away after the healing. (It's worth noting that Jesus seemed to have gone to the pool not for a mass healing service, but for *this one man*.)

8. People who were sick and disabled were considered unclean under Jewish law and therefore were unable to enter the temple. Why do you think it was significant for him to go to the temple?

Jesus wasn't concerned only with the man's physical healing but with his spiritual healing as well! Jesus sought him out again, but the second time it was to ensure he understood that the eternal consequences of sin are far worse than the inability to walk.

We don't know what the man's motivation was, but he went back to tell the religious leaders that it was Jesus who had healed him. The leaders were more focused on what Jesus had "broken" than on what He had healed. Jesus's reply to their shortsightedness was a doozy! He claimed unity and Sonship with God, and He insisted that God was at work, so it was perfectly natural for Him to be working too. Jesus hadn't broken anything. He was in the business of healing and restoring!

John 5:18–29

 READ JOHN 5:18–29

1. Review 5:16–18.

The stage was set; Jesus's showdown with the religious leaders had officially begun. Jesus had been breaking the Pharisees' Sabbath traditions, saying God was on His side of the debate, and claiming that God was His own Father! The religious leaders didn't miss that Jesus was claiming equality with God; they became fully committed to putting a stop to Him—and they knew that meant putting Him to death.

2. Review 5:19–24. Why do you think the religious leaders were so offended by Jesus's claim of unity with the Father?

Jesus's words in 5:19 can be easy to misunderstand. He was using standard rabbinical language in His reply to these religious leaders. He tied His work on the Sabbath to His submission to the Father's will and work. He wasn't functioning as a subordinate, but as an equal who was filling a unique role in their divine plan. God the Father and God the Son are equal in power, but they carry out different roles in the process of salvation for those He adopts into His family. Unity between the Father and Son is foundational to God's plan for His creation—for judgment or for eternal life.

Since most of us aren't familiar with the structure of first-century rabbinical oration, it may seem like Jesus took a hard left turn when He brought up judgment in 5:22. But Jesus was just giving another example of the division of labor between the Father and Son (by the way, God the Spirit is also a part of this plan and division of labor; that's just not covered in this particular text). While the Father has power over life and death, the Son was given the role of judge.

3. According to 5:23, why does Jesus have the role of judge?

The Father has authority over life and death, and the Son has authority over judgment. Together they share authority over the eternal lives of those who hear and respond to the message of the Son.

4. Look at 5:24 again. How does this reveal that information about God doesn't always lead to heart transformation? Have you found that to be true in your own life? If so, describe.

5. Review 5:25–29.

In 5:25, Jesus said even the dead would hear His voice and live eternally. He may have been speaking of those who were physically dead, but it's far more likely that He was speaking of those who were spiritually dead. Either way, it's a feat only God could fulfill!

6. Given what we've learned so far, use a Bible commentary to write 5:26–27 into your own words.

Jesus told His listeners that His authority extended beyond the temporal and into the eternal. Every human has an eternity ahead of them, so the weight of 5:28–29 cannot be overstated. According to Jesus, a time will come when every person will have to give an account of their life before God.

7. Read Hebrews 4:13. How is this verse comforting to you? How is this verse convicting to you?

In 5:29, Jesus said that the eternity waiting for those who have done good is life, and the eternity waiting for those who have done evil is judgment. What Jesus was *not* saying was that salvation is based on works. Jesus repeatedly made it clear that belief in Him was the only path to eternal life. But as Jesus's brother James clarified in James 2, faith without works is dead.

Tomorrow we'll dig into the second half of Jesus's conversation with the rabbis, where He further explained His own divinity.

John 5:30–47

 READ JOHN 5:30–47

1. Review 5:30–32.

2. Read Deuteronomy 19:15. According to Jewish law, how many witnesses were required for something to be proven as true? How does this information clarify the meaning of 5:31?

In today's reading, Jesus laid out an entire case before the religious rulers to prove He is the Son sent from the Father. It's as if Jesus were presenting arguments before a grand jury. So we'll approach today's study by exploring the legal nature of this text.

3. Review 5:33–47.

4. In 5:32, Jesus said He had witnesses to support His relationship with the Father. Even though He only needed two or three witnesses, He provided five. Match the verse with who or what bore witness about His divinity.

5:33–35	Moses
5:36	Scriptures
5:37–38	JTB
5:39	Works of Jesus
5:45–47	Father

Jesus's first witness was His cousin, JTB. Jesus didn't need the testimony of JTB, but He knew His audience did. They knew who JTB was, and Jesus even implied that they were willing to listen to him and liked what he had to say . . . for a little while. JTB brought the truth to light, but they refused to see it.

The second witness was the physical evidence of Jesus's miracles. This was an even greater witness than JTB because it couldn't be disputed! In doing the Father's work, Jesus demonstrated more than just His power—He demonstrated His divinity. But as we read earlier this week, the religious leaders were more concerned with their man-made laws being broken than with the miracles.

The third trial witness was the Father Himself.

5. What four accusations did Jesus list against the religious leaders in conjunction with His third witness? Fill in the blanks from 5:37–38.

His _____ you have never _____.

His _____ you have never _____.

You do not have _____ _____ _____ in _____.

You do not _____ the _____ whom He has _____.

It makes sense that Jesus said the Scriptures were about Him, because He'd already established God as His witness, and God and the Scriptures never disagree. What a powerful fourth witness to use in an argument with the religious scholars!

6. When Jesus referred to the Scriptures, what was He talking about?

These men prided themselves on their knowledge of Scripture and their ability to interpret its meaning. In their finite human understanding, they thought the highest calling from God was to know and keep the Mosaic law to the letter. They sought salvation through their own good deeds. No wonder they were so prideful.

The things Jesus said in 5:40–43 all built toward His main argument against His accusers in 5:44. Jesus had cleanly laid out a legal case, but He knew they wouldn't accept it.

7. Why wouldn't the religious elite believe? Fill in the table below.

Verse	Jesus's Accusation of Religious Rulers
5:40	
5:41	
5:42	
5:43b	

In 5:44, Jesus summed up all the reasons with one key factor: pride. These religious men were willing to trade honor from God for the immediate gratification of honor from each other. In Charles Spurgeon's sermon "Why Men Cannot Believe in Christ," he said, "When a man gets to feel that he ought to be honoured, he is in extreme danger."* When appearing impressive to others supersedes our need to honor the Lord, we begin to make compromises we never expected to make. We may end up depending on others for something that can only come from the Father.

---

*Charles Haddon Spurgeon, "Why Men Cannot Believe in Christ," Metropolitan Tabernacle Pulpit, vol. 21, https://www.spurgeon.org/resource-library/sermons/why-men-cannot-believe-in-christ.

8. Think of a time when you sought approval from people over approval from God. What was the outcome?

Even though He had surpassed the two-to-three-witness threshold of the Old Testament law, He brought a surprise witness at the end. An accusation from Jesus held no weight for them because they didn't care what Jesus thought. But they certainly cared about the opinion of Moses. Moses gave them God's law, and it was the law that these so-called elite looked to for salvation.

9. Why would Moses accuse the religious leaders to the Father? Look up 5:45–47 in a commentary for help.

These men had built their lives on Moses's words. They must have skipped over what Moses said in Deuteronomy 18:15, "The LORD your God will raise up for you a prophet like me from among you, from your brothers—it is to him you shall listen." Moses knew Jesus would come, and he wanted everyone to listen to Jesus, because He's where the joy is.

10. What stood out to you most in this week's study? Why?

11. What did you learn or relearn about God and His character this week?

Corresponding Psalm & Prayer

 READ PSALM 36

1. What correlation do you see between Psalm 36 and this week's study of Jesus as God?

2. What portions of this psalm stand out to you most?

3. Close by praying this prayer aloud:

Father,
*   "Your steadfast love . . . extends to the heavens and your faithful-*
ness to the clouds" (Psalm 36:5). You are powerful and good and
kind; You care perfectly for Your kids.

Like the Pharisees, I've cared more about appearances than actual obedience. I have sought my own glory. I have chased the approval of others. I have been so obsessed with proving my own righteousness that I've missed the miracle of Your steadfast love.

Remind me when I drink that You are the fountain of life. Remind me when I eat that You invite me to feast abundantly. Remind me when I lie down that You are my refuge. Remind me when I wake that You are the Light. May my everyday actions point me to eternal truths.

Whatever You've promised, I believe. Wherever You're leading, I'll go. I surrender my life to You, Lord—every moment of my day, each decision I make, I yield my will and way to Your perfect will and way.

I love You too. Amen.

Rest, Catch Up, or Dig Deeper

 WEEKLY CHALLENGE

On Day 5, we read about how Jesus built a case before the religious leaders, explaining His relationship to the Father. Scripture encourages us to always be "prepared to make a defense to anyone who asks you for a reason for the hope that is in you; yet do it with gentleness and respect" (1 Peter 3:15). Many people don't believe the truth because the truth has never been explained to them. This week, choose an apologetics question and research the answer so you can grow in your understanding of the truth. Try to use at least three trusted resources in your process.

John 6–7
The Sovereignty of God

DAILY BIBLE READING

Day 1: John 6:1–21

Day 2: John 6:22–59

Day 3: John 6:60–71

Day 4: John 7:1–31

Day 5: John 7:32–52

Day 6: Psalm 139

Day 7: Catch-Up Day

Corresponds to Days 291 and 296 of *The Bible Recap*.

WEEKLY CHALLENGE

See page 84 for more information.

John 6:1–21

 READ JOHN 6:1–21

Today's reading takes place during the second Passover mentioned in John's gospel. The two big miracles in this passage represent numbers four and five of Jesus's seven public signs, and they may be familiar to you. If you went to Sunday school as a kid, you probably saw them on the felt board. As an adult, you've likely seen them in paintings. Even people unfamiliar with the Bible have heard of Jesus walking on water or feeding the five thousand. But sometimes familiarity can stifle our awe and tempt us to skim over noteworthy details. Hebrews 4:12, however, says God's Word is living and active—so whether it's your first or fiftieth time reading these miracles, let's experience them with fresh eyes today.

1. Review 6:1–15.

2. Which disciple does Jesus ask about the bread? Why does He ask him?

Have you ever wondered what was going on in Philip's heart and mind that made Jesus specifically ask *him*? Jesus wasn't asking Philip to think of the best grocery store or come up with a brilliant strategy. He was taking an opportunity to draw Philip's attention to His heart and His power.

And how kind of Jesus! Amid the task of feeding five thousand men (which means that the number of people fed that day, including women and children, was likely at least fifteen thousand) and amid grieving the death of His cousin (Matthew 14:12 reveals Jesus learned of it right before this event), Jesus still took the time to teach Philip something personal.

3. They basically started with one Lunchables. How much did they have left over?

    A. None. They had exactly enough for everyone and no more.

    B. Five handfuls.

    C. We aren't told.

    D. Twelve baskets full. The same number as the number of disciples.

    E. The exact amount they started with.

4. If you were a disciple, how soon into gathering the leftovers do you think your heart would start to quicken? How did the crowd respond in 6:14–15?

5. **Review 6:16–21.**

Jesus withdrew to the mountain. And after all the day's challenges and excitement, the disciples ran into a storm. This area on the Sea of Galilee is situated by a valley that basically acts like a wind tunnel, so the area is known for sudden and unexpected storms. And because He had told them to get into the boat (Matthew 14:22–23), surely some of them were thinking, *Jesus, You told us to be here! And now we're stuck rowing our arms off in a storm?* It can be easy to interpret "storms" in life as a sign we're doing something wrong—or to assume that if we're obedient, everything will go right. But their obedience was what led them right into the middle of the storm.

6. Can you relate to this? If so, how?

7. Write Jesus's words from 6:20 below.

Picture Jesus saying those words. Jesus walking on water was a huge deal, and we might be tempted to breeze past the other amazing part of this miraculous moment: They survived the storm and landed safely at the shore. When our jobs seem too hard and our shores seem too far off, we want to be delivered from the storm, but sometimes He delivers us *through* it instead.

8. Look back at the words above you wrote from 6:20. Then, write out a short prayer asking God to remind you of His nearness to you in whatever circumstances feel like a storm.

John 6:22–59

 READ JOHN 6:22–59

Today's reading takes place the day after Jesus fed fifteen thousand people and walked on water. The crowd who witnessed yesterday's miracle was desperately trying to track Jesus down again.

1. Review 6:22–27.

2. What did the crowd say to Jesus in 6:25?

They had seen His disciples get into the boats the night before, and they knew Jesus hadn't gone with them. The crowd searched all along the shoreline, moving north from Tiberias. When they got to Capernaum and found Jesus there, they were confused. *Wait, how'd He get here? Is there a shortcut?*

Without even addressing His miraculous overnight adventure, He moved straight into some strong words for the crowd. He accused them of following Him because of the food He provided, not because they believed the signs of His divinity. They wanted freebies, not faith. They'd come face-to-face with the Messiah and missed the entire point. As they listened, they had an important follow-up question.

3. **Review 6:28–29.** How do you think most people today would answer this question?

4. But how did Jesus answer in 6:29?

Do we really believe that? That the *work* is to *believe*? Jesus didn't say belief is the icing on the cake of good works. He said the work *is* belief. This revelation was an invitation to rely on the one who would perfectly complete all that the Father required. Jesus was offering them freedom from trying to earn their salvation in a culture that was entirely built around keeping the law.

5. What does Ephesians 2:8–9 tell us?

   A. Salvation is earned through our works.

   B. Salvation is not earned through our works.

   C. Those that earn salvation may boast.

   D. Salvation is the gift of God.

   E. C and D

   F. B and D

Paul's letter to the church at Ephesus echoes the words of Jesus in today's reading. How freeing! And in another of Paul's letters—to the church at Philippi—he doubles down on this peace-inducing truth, pointing out that belief is *also* granted to us by God (Philippians 1:29). That's important to remember. If you're tempted to misunderstand Jesus's answer here and take it to mean that moments of doubt or unbelief will make God reject you, remember that He's kind enough to meet you in that space. He knows we're often like the man in Mark 9:24 who said, "I believe; help my unbelief!"

6. Where do you struggle with unbelief in your own heart? Write out a prayer inspired by Mark 9:24, addressing those areas. Commit to resisting doubt when it tries to have the final word.

7. Review 6:30–59.

As for the crowd, they didn't understand. They wanted Him to prove He was worth believing in. They even went so far as to suggest He do a miraculous work like Moses had done and provide bread for them. (He just did that for them yesterday, which was why they followed Him!) He told them Moses, whom they revered, didn't do that sign on his own—God was the source and the goal of it.

Then, Jesus turned the whole conversation: Not only was God the *source* of bread, but Jesus was God and He *was* the bread, the very supply they needed. When Jesus said, "I am the bread of life," it was the first of His seven metaphorical *I am* statements in the book of John, which we talked about in the introduction. That statement—*I am*—connects to His deity, pointing back to the name God used to refer to Himself when He spoke to Moses. Jesus revealed that He was united with the will and plan of the Father.

Then, as if His statement weren't radical enough, He dialed up the intensity twice more. First, He referred to Himself as the Son of Man, the long-awaited Messiah. He previously made this claim when Nicodemus came to Him by night (John 3:13–14), but here He made it publicly, for all to hear. Then, he said they must eat His flesh and drink His blood—a shocking idea regardless of whether you take it in the physical sense or the spiritual sense. And the crowd was appalled. After all, eating flesh and drinking blood was not only disgusting, but against their laws! But Jesus had a different story in mind—one that connects to the old covenant, where the priests offered the same sacrifices day after day.

Hebrews 10:11 says those sacrifices could never take away sins. But Jesus said His flesh and blood would be the once-for-all-time sacrifice that would end the need for daily sacrifices. It would be complete in His death and resurrection.

8. In 6:51, what does Jesus promise to anyone who eats this bread?

John 6:60–71

 READ JOHN 6:60-71

Yesterday's reading ended with Jesus introducing the idea of eating His flesh and drinking His blood. We can recognize now that He was referring to Communion. He was pointing to what He would do on the cross, sacrificing His body and blood for our salvation. But we have the benefit of hindsight. The initial hearers when Jesus said this hadn't yet heard of Communion, and they hadn't yet seen Him on the cross. It logically follows that many of the disciples struggled with what Jesus said here.

1. Review 6:60–65.

2. In a Bible lexicon, look up the original Greek words John used in 6:60 for "hard saying." Write those words and their definitions below.

The implication here is not that Jesus's words were hard to understand—it's that they were hard to accept. Jesus knew it was a tough saying, and He let them know that there were *more* shocking things to come.

3. What do you think Jesus was referring to in 6:62? Use a Bible commentary for help if you need it.

It's almost as if Jesus was preaching a space-making sermon here—emptying out the seats of the fair-weather followers—because He not only told them that one of them would betray Him, but that their flesh was useless in their efforts at righteousness, and that none of them could follow Him unless God had appointed it. Some of them may have wondered, *Has God granted it to me to follow Jesus?* And for those whom God had granted it, they stayed. But many others stopped following Jesus after that point. Imagine how heartbreaking—Jesus revealed His identity and that He was the source of life, yet they walked away.

4. Review 6:66–71.

5. Circle the names of the twelve (bearing in mind some disciples were known by multiple names or nicknames):

Lewis	Andrew	James	John the Baptist	John who wrote this gospel	
Philip	Thomas	Nicodemus	Matthew	James the son of Alpheus	Thaddeus
Jacob	Simon the Zealot	Simon Peter	Luke	Judas Iscariot	Bartholomew

Today's passage made a distinction between two different types of disciples: those who left and those who remained.

6. Look up the word *disciple* in a Greek lexicon and write what you find below.

In addition to the chosen twelve disciples, Jesus had other disciples, with varying degrees of devotion to His ministry, who followed Him around. But as some walked away, He asked Simon Peter a piercing question.

7. What was Simon Peter's response to Jesus in 6:68?

8. Can you think of a time when that sentiment (*This is hard. But where else would I go? You're the only one who speaks the words of life.*) has been your own? If so, describe.

Remember, John's gospel is constantly pointing us back to the beginning and pointing to Jesus as God.

9. How did the book begin? Fill in the blanks from John 1:1:

In the beginning was the _____, and the _____ was with God, and _____ _____ _____ _____.

The Word was God. Jesus was that Word. Peter got it. He said, "We have believed, and have come to know, that you are the Holy One of God." Though many left Jesus that day, He knew that one of those who remained was not really a believer.

It's easy to blow past this. Even in pop culture, we'll hear someone being called a "Judas," meaning they're a traitor. But imagine you're one of the twelve, and after all this time of being on the road with Jesus, leaving your homes and families to travel together, you hear, "One of you is a devil." *What?* Think about what this would have been like.

Imagine the courage, the patience, the perseverance of Jesus to look His betrayer in the eye, knowing *from the beginning* that he would betray Him—and to invite him to follow anyway.

John 7:1–31

 READ JOHN 7:1–31

It's festival time in Judea—the Feast of Tabernacles. This was one of three annual feasts when Jews from all over Israel traveled to Jerusalem to celebrate.

1. Review 7:1–9.

Jesus's brothers were mocking Him. They didn't believe He was the Messiah, so it's probably fair to say Jesus had His share of family drama. This is both shocking and heartbreaking for us to read—*how could they not know?*—but if it's any comfort, at least two of Jesus's brothers (James and Jude) are credited with writing books of the Bible, which means they had a change of heart.

2. How did James introduce himself in James 1:1?

James, a _____ of God and of ____ _____ _____ _____.

His doubting brother later became such a servant to Jesus that it was how he introduced himself!

3. Was there a time when you doubted the divinity of Jesus? If so, describe what it took to get you past that uncertainty.

4. Review 7:10–13.

Imagine glimpsing the Son of God, but, for fear of man, not saying anything. It's important to note here that Jesus didn't go back on His word when He told His brothers He wasn't going. The phrase Jesus used in the Greek often means "yet," as in, "not *yet* going."

5. Write down the two primary opinions of Jesus from 7:12.

- Some said:

- Others said:

How do both of these opinions fall short?

6. Review 7:14–24. In this section and the one that follows, Jesus draws clear connections to His divinity, showing His intimate relationship with the Father. Match the verses below with the things Jesus says He shares with the Father.

7:16		His origin / sending
7:17–18		His teaching
7:28–29		His authority

The people didn't believe Jesus's teaching or miracles were from God, so Jesus sought to establish the unity He has with the Father. They also misunderstood the purposes of God's laws, accusing Jesus of breaking the law by healing on the Sabbath. Jesus reasoned with them, showing how their understanding was irrational.

7. In 7:23, what comparison did Jesus use to show it wasn't sinful for Him to heal on the Sabbath?

8. Fill in the blanks from 7:24 below.

_____ _____ _____ by appearances, but _____ with _____

_____

9. What do you think it means to judge rightly?

It's interesting to note that He didn't tell them *not* to judge Him. The people seemed eager to challenge the works of Jesus without thinking things through, but He encouraged them to use wisdom in their judgment. Our modern culture latches onto biblical phrases like "judge not," but Jesus encouraged wise judgment, which would've required the crowds to pay attention not only to the details of the law but to the heart of God behind establishing the law. These nuances are important.

10. Review 7:25–31.

The people wondered if Jesus was the Christ, then doubted because of "what they knew" in 7:27.

11. Read Micah 5:2 and circle the prophecy it references.

    A. No one would know where the Messiah was born.

    B. The Messiah would be born in Bethlehem.

    C. The Messiah would be born in an undisclosed location.

    D. The Messiah would be born in an unnamed city.

What they dissuaded themselves with wasn't even biblical! It was just a popular saying. Apparently, confusing cultural sayings with biblical truth isn't just something we struggle with today—it's a problem that has been around for a long time.

12. Why were they unable to arrest Jesus in 7:30? What do you think this means? Use a Bible commentary for help.

We end today's reading with the encouraging news that many people had begun to develop a curious faith in Jesus—and while they may not have been fully settled on His divinity, they were willing to seek the truth!

John 7:32–52

 READ JOHN 7:32–52

Today's passage picks up where we left off yesterday: Jesus teaching in the temple at the Feast of Tabernacles.

1. Review 7:32–36.

As the crowds continued muttering about Jesus, the Pharisees decided to take action. They escalated their plan and sent officers to arrest Him. In 7:33–34, He wasn't suggesting that they'd be unable to arrest Him but was communicating things on a grander scale—addressing God's plan for His impending death, resurrection, and ascension to heaven. These prophetic statements were impossible for them to understand at the time, but Jesus's words proved true.

2. Reread 7:34—"You will seek me and you will not find me. Where I am you cannot come." In the table, circle the correct verb tenses.

You will seek	Past	Present	Future
You will not find	Past	Present	Future
Where I am	Past	Present	Future

This can be a challenging concept to grasp. But remember, John is the gospel that most specifically displays Jesus as God. And here we have another reminder of that truth. Though Jesus was physically present with this crowd as a human male, He is also the God who exists outside of time.

3. **Review 7:37–39.**

There's an interesting note about the timeline of the Feast of Tabernacles, but it's lost without an understanding of the timeline and history. This feast is also called Sukkot, and it takes place in the seventh month of the Jewish calendar—now known as Tishrei, which means "beginning." However, before the Jewish calendar got a little mixed up during the Babylonian exile, the seventh month was called something else.

4. What does 1 Kings 8:2 tell us the seventh month was called?

This name means "waters flowing steadily" and "perpetual rivers that do not run dry."* Hold on to that thought as we examine what Jesus said on this last and greatest day of the feast.

5. Circle every word that relates to water in 7:37–38:

> "If anyone thirsts, let him come to me and drink. Whoever believes in me, as the Scripture has said, 'Out of his heart will flow rivers of living water.'"

Jesus said this about the Holy Spirit, who had not yet been given to them. And He said it on the eighth and final day of the feast. During the first seven feast days, water was poured out on the altar to remind them of the water God miraculously provided for Israel in the wilderness. But on the eighth day, tradition held that there would be no pouring of the water—there would be only *prayers* for water. Jesus's timing was profound—He was telling them He is the fulfillment of that prayer!

---

*See "H388 - 'ytnym – Strong's Hebrew Lexicon (kjv)," Blue Letter Bible, accessed 5 July, 2024, https://www.blueletterbible.org/lexicon/h388/kjv/wlc/0-1.

6. Review 7:40–52.

Again, the crowd began to debate whether Jesus was the Messiah, basing their arguments on His birthplace. But this time, their arguments held a bit more accuracy: Yes, He was born in Bethlehem, as Scripture prophesied, and yes, He came to Jerusalem from Galilee, where He lived at the time.

As the Pharisees sought to arrest Him, they ended up in another debate with the officers, who found His words compelling and unique. The Pharisees, however, relied on the logic that if none of their peers believed in Jesus, that spoke for itself. But there was one among them who seemed to believe, or was at least moving closer to belief.

7. What familiar name appears in 7:50? What do you think motivated him to say what he said?

The chief priests and the Pharisees pushed back, but it seems the truth had already started to take root in Nicodemus's heart. Perhaps he had begun to see and believe the beautiful truth about Jesus—that He's where the joy is!

8. What stood out to you most in this week's study? Why?

9. What did you learn or relearn about God and His character this week?

Corresponding Psalm & Prayer

 READ PSALM 139

1. What correlation do you see between Psalm 139 and this week's study of Jesus as God?

2. What portions of this psalm stand out to you most?

3. Close by praying this prayer aloud:

Father,
    My soul knows well that Your thoughts are precious and Your works are wonderful! You walked on the very waters You created.

You fed the crowds with food You made grow. You fulfilled every prophecy You gave in Your Word.

You have searched me and You know me, and You know that I'm misled by voices that aren't Yours; I'm swayed by arrogance and pride. I'm deceived by thoughts You didn't give; I fixate on doubt and fear. I've walked in the way of popular opinion, short-term pleasures, empty praise, and fruitless striving.

Lord, search my heart again, and lead me to repentance. Turn my thoughts to Your thoughts. Tune my ear to Your voice. Lead me in the everlasting way.

You are sovereign over every detail that ever was or will be. You've numbered the days of everything and everyone You created. You're acquainted with all my ways, words, and thoughts. You know me and You know what's best for me. I trust You, and I submit to You.

I surrender my life to You, Lord—every moment of my day, each decision I make, I yield my will and way to Your perfect will and way.

I love You too. Amen.

Rest, Catch Up, or Dig Deeper

 WEEKLY CHALLENGE

This week's study covers many moments when the fear of man kept people from voicing the truth, and when not knowing what God's Word really said left people vulnerable. Create an art piece—perhaps a drawing or a collage—showing all the outside voices that tend to affect your thoughts and decisions. In the center of the piece, show yourself being surrounded by the truth of God's Word. Let it serve as a visible reminder of where your strength comes from.

┌─ Scripture to Memorize ─┐

Abide in me, and I in you. As
the branch cannot bear fruit
by itself, unless it abides in
the vine, neither can you,
unless you abide in me.

John 15:4

John 8–9
The Light of God

DAILY BIBLE READING

Day 1: John 8:1–30 (and 7:53)
Day 2: John 8:31–47
Day 3: John 8:48–59
Day 4: John 9:1–23
Day 5: John 9:24–41
Day 6: Psalm 27
Day 7: Catch-Up Day

Corresponds to Days 296–297 of *The Bible Recap.*

WEEKLY CHALLENGE

See page 106 for more information.

John 8:1–30 (and 7:53)

 READ JOHN 8:1–30 (AND 7:53)

Your Bible likely had a note before today's reading that 7:53–8:11 wasn't included in original manuscripts. There are two possible reasons why: Some believe that a scribe who knew the story inserted it while making a copy, while others explain that the early church didn't want any misconceptions that Jesus approved of promiscuity. But even though this account isn't recorded in any other gospel, historians and theologians alike agree that it is accurate. It's also important to note that the events and message in this passage don't conflict with anything Jesus did or taught; rather, the passage is consistent with His words and actions elsewhere. With that said, today's story began in the outer courts of the temple, where Jewish teachers often taught their students.

1. Review 7:53–8:11. What did the scribes and Pharisees do in 8:3–4? What did they want?

For what wasn't the first time—and what wouldn't be the last time—the leaders set a trap for Jesus. If He told the accusers to stone the woman, they could report Him to the Roman authorities for calling for an execution without their approval. If He said to let her go, they could bring a case against Him to the religious authorities for ignoring the law of Moses.

2. **Read Leviticus 20:10 and Deuteronomy 22:22.** Did the accusers follow the law? Why or why not?

Many of us read this passage and wonder what Jesus wrote. Whether it was letters, words, or drawings, the Bible doesn't tell us. So instead of asking what Jesus wrote, let's turn our attention to a different question: What did Jesus *do*?

This woman, as we learned in 8:3, was caught *in the act* of adultery and dragged through bustling Jerusalem to a crowd gathered to hear Jesus teach. Since the Pharisees' purpose was to exploit this woman to entrap Jesus, and since forced public nudity was a weaponized method of shame in ancient cultures, it's likely that she was still naked, dragged from the place where they found her. Already terrified and humiliated, now the woman heard that they planned to kill her in a slow and painful way.

Jesus often dignified people by looking at them or touching them. But this time, He dignified her by looking *away*. While He was crouched down, writing in the sand, the eyes of the crowd went from glaring at the woman to watching Jesus with curiosity.

3. What does this tell you about the heart of Jesus?

Jesus didn't condemn the woman, but He didn't condone her actions either. He was the only righteous person in the crowd—the only one who could've met His qualification of being without sin. And though He could've righteously cast judgment on her for her sin, He extended mercy. He rescued her from the murderous mob, and when she encountered His radical mercy, He told her to go and "sin no more" (8:11).

4. Review 8:12–30. Referencing 8:12, fill in the blanks below.

Again Jesus spoke to them, saying, "I am _____ _____ _____ _____

_____. Whoever follows me will not walk in _____, but will have the

_____ of _____."

This is the second metaphorical *I am* statement in John, and with it Jesus compared Himself to light. Darkness often symbolizes death, despair, or depravity. Just as John wrote in the opening of his gospel, Jesus is light: life, hope, and goodness. And here, He said that He was the light not only of the Jewish people, but *of the world*. Boldly, He declared His divine identity while also acknowledging that God's plan involved more than just the Jews. The Pharisees, who were likely growing in their offense, continued their dispute with Him, trying to outsmart God Himself.

5. What was the Pharisees' accusation against Jesus? What was Jesus's response?

Since His time on earth, those who don't believe in Jesus have made false assumptions about Him. Some view Him as a subversive traitor. Others think He was simply insane. But in this section, Jesus affirmed His identity as the Son of God (8:19) *and* His identity as God the Son (8:29).

6. Jesus revealed a lot about Himself, but also about His hearers. In the table below, draw lines matching each verse with what it reveals in both columns.

Truths about Jesus	Verse	Truths about His Hearers
He is from above	8:14b	They will understand His identity after He is crucified
Knowledge of Jesus is knowledge of the Father	8:19	They will look for Jesus after He goes away
He acts and speaks on the Father's authority	8:21	They don't know Jesus or the Father
He knows where He came from and is going	8:23	They are from below
Jesus is going somewhere they can't go	8:28	They don't know where He came from or is going

The closer Jesus got to His death, the more He encountered skeptics, critics, and those scheming to kill Him. And as He often did, He offered them the invitation to repent and believe in Him (8:24). And as He spoke, "many believed in Him" (8:30). Praise God for those before us who believed, spreading the good news of great joy that's made its way around the world and across generations to us today!

John 8:31–47

 READ JOHN 8:31–47

1. Review 8:31–38. In the ESV, this section heading is "The Truth Will Set You Free." How have you heard this phrase used or misused?

Hold on to your answer; we'll revisit it shortly. Jesus taught His audience that abiding in His word would lead to them knowing the truth, which would lead to them being set free. They thought He meant they'd be set free from an earthly master, but their response is baffling. These people who were descendants of slaves and who were under Rome's oppressive rule claimed they were a people who had always been free. Perhaps this same delusion caused some of them—eyewitnesses to the earthly ministry of Jesus—to be blind to His divinity as God the Son.

In contrast to this delusion, Jesus painted a picture of genuine faith. To abide in Jesus is to actively believe and continually do what He says. Real faith is permanent and growing; it's transformational and lasting.

When we read Jesus's words about slavery, it's important to remember that slavery in the first century was different from slavery as we think of it today. At that time, people willingly entered servitude for a specified length of time to pay back debt. When that period of time expired, an honest master would release slaves from his household and send them back to their homes. (While this is clearly different from the forced slavery we're familiar with, it's important to note that Jesus didn't condone slavery.)

But His point is as true for us today as it was for His original hearers: We're all slaves to sin, and Jesus is our only hope for freedom. Sin lies, steals, destroys, and kills.

2. Reread 8:32 and 8:36. Then fill in the blanks below.

"And you will know the _____, and the _____ will set you free" (8:32).

"So if the _____ sets you free, you will be free indeed" (8:36).

Remember our first question of the day? When Jesus said, "The truth will set you free," He was talking about *Himself*. Do not cheapen the profound theological reality Jesus taught here. He wasn't making a cultural or political statement then, and we shouldn't interpret it as one now. It's not a catchphrase we should use to affirm our personal preferences or to belittle those who don't agree with us. It's a tenet of the gospel: *He* is the truth, and *He* frees us. He frees us from the guilt and shame caused by sin and from its power to control us. He frees us to truth, obedience, and righteousness.

3. Read Romans 6:15–18. Use Paul's teaching to fill in the table below.

What were we slaves to?		What are we slaves to now?
	". . . but thanks be to God . . ."	

Jesus made it clear that His Father was not their father. The unbelieving people in His audience told Him that their father was Abraham, but Jesus confirmed that while they were descendants of Abraham, they were not children of Abraham (8:37). True children of Abraham are faithful followers of God, which means they believe in Jesus.

4. In 8:38, what was Jesus implying about those who don't believe in Him?

5. Review 8:39–47.

Jesus was the perfect representation of His Father: every word, every ac-tion, and every thought was sinless. The Pharisees were also a representa-tion of *their* father, the father of lies: the devil. If this seems harsh, let's review their track record in John 8 alone: They attempted to trap Jesus to turn Him over to Roman or religious authorities (8:6); they publicly chal-lenged His teaching and implied He was lying (8:13); they were actively looking for a way to kill Him (8:37). And as if that wasn't enough, they came after His mom, insinuating that the virgin birth was adultery (8:41).

6. In 8:43, what explanation did Jesus give as to why the Pharisees didn't understand Him?

Just as darkness cannot bear the light, lies cannot bear the truth. Since the beginning, the devil has been a liar and a murderer. He tempted Eve to try the fruit, and he motivated Cain to kill Abel. And he continued his work through the Pharisees, prompting them to attempt to destroy Jesus. The father of lies has always delighted in destruction, but the Father of creation is sovereign, and nothing ever has—or ever will—happen outside of His plan.

7. Read Revelation 12:12. When it comes to the devil, what can we be sure of?

DAY 3

John 8:48–59

READ JOHN 8:48-59

For the last two days, we've studied the religious leaders' arguments against Jesus, and His teachings in response. Their discussion concluded today with Jesus's most profound—and inflammatory—statement of truth, one that led to an attempted execution.

1. Review 8:48–51.

Yesterday, we read that Jesus publicly called the Pharisees what they were, sons of the devil. Today, we opened with their reply: They accused Jesus of being a Samaritan and having a demon. As you probably learned in your research during week 2, Samaritans were half Jewish and were viewed as inferior and unclean. So after insulting His mom, the Pharisees tried to insult Jesus. And then, by asking if He had a demon, they implied He was insane.

Again, Jesus explained who He is and why He came.

2. Use a Bible study tool to read 8:51 in each of the translations below. List the assurance Jesus spoke at the beginning of the verse in each version. Then fill in the promise Jesus made.

Translation	Assurance	Condition	Promise
ESV	Truly, truly		
NIV			
NLT		*if anyone keeps my word,*	
NKJV			

No matter how you say it, the assurance is secure and the promise is sure: Those who follow Jesus will never see death. Death—the shared fate of every human who has ever lived—has nothing on God. Its defeat could only have been promised with such certainty by the one with the power to conquer it: God Himself. Jesus was speaking of salvation from spiritual death, and He also was speaking about the fact that He would someday abolish physical death. When He comes again, He will defeat death altogether!

3. Review 8:52–59.

The Jewish leaders doubled down on their claim that He was insane, insisting that all this talk about defeating death meant He was definitely demon-possessed. They said that even Abraham—the father of the Jewish people—died, so of course they would all die too. After they essentially asked Jesus who on earth He thought He was, Jesus told them something amazing about Abraham.

4. Read Genesis 22:9–14 and Hebrews 11:3. How would you explain what Jesus meant when He said, "Abraham rejoiced that he would see my day. He saw it and was glad" (8:56)?

The Pharisees mocked Him, saying He wasn't even fifty years old, so there was no possible way He had seen Abraham. They were blind to the fact that—by limiting Him with something as finite as age—they were mocking the very Creator of time and the only one who is outside of it.

And then, as they continued to argue against Him, Jesus dropped His biggest divine truth yet.

5. Complete His statement from 8:58 below.

   Jesus said to them, "Truly, truly, I say to you, before Abraham was, ___
   _____."

6. Now read Exodus 3:14 and complete God's statement to Moses below.

   God said to Moses, "_____ _____ _____ _____ _____."

In addition to the metaphorical *I am*'s in John, there are also absolute *I am*'s, and this is a major one. God the Son used the same language with the unbelieving religious leaders that God the Father used with the then-scared Moses.

With the stories he tells and the teaching he recounts, John keeps taking us all the way back to the beginning. Jesus has been here all along: before Abraham, the father of the Israelites, and before Moses, who led them out of slavery. And not only has He been here all along, eternally existent, but He's been here *as God* all along, eternally divine.

7. What do John 8:58 and Exodus 3:14 tell us about God's character? Use a Bible commentary if you need help getting started.

The Pharisees thought Jesus using God's divine name was blasphemy, so they picked up rocks to stone Him—though of course they ignored the law they claimed to love by not conducting a trial first.

Jesus would soon die, and then He would defeat death. But His time had not yet come, so He "hid himself" (8:59) and escaped from their vigilante violence to continue to do His work.

John 9:1–23

 READ JOHN 9:1-23

1. *Review 9:1–5.*

In the first century, a common cultural belief was that sickness and disability were caused by sin. We see this in the disciples' question to Jesus in 9:2: "Rabbi, who sinned, this man or his parents, that he was born blind?" We may be tempted to chalk this up to an antiquated understanding of science, but this belief still exists today, whether we realize it or not. Think about how you've heard Christians respond to their brothers and sisters having miscarriages, relapsing with cancer, or struggling with anxiety or depression. While some sins absolutely have physical consequences, most sickness—and certainly disability—is the result of living in a fallen world.

2. In 9:3, how did Jesus respond to His disciples' misguided understanding? Fill in the blanks below.

"It was _____ that this man _____, or his _____, but that the _____ of _____ might be _____ in him."

Though Jesus's primary work during His time on earth was teaching, He also used miracles and healings to underscore His message. And out of all the recorded healings, the most frequent type is giving sight to the blind, bringing them from literal darkness into light. So it's no small thing that in 9:5, He again called Himself "the light of the world."

3. Review 9:6–7. What did Jesus do and say to heal the blind man?

The pool of Siloam was built inside Jerusalem's city walls during the reign of King Hezekiah. The pool likely got its name because it held water that was "sent" into the city from outside. And Jesus sent a blind man there to receive his sight.

The pool itself was massive—about four times the size of an Olympic pool. Archaeologists first uncovered it in 2004, and excavations have continued for decades. It was a safe and convenient place to get water, which meant that on any given day, many people would've gathered there.

4. How was sending the blind man to this crowded pool a shift from His previous public signs, like when He healed the nobleman's son or the man at Bethesda?

5. Review 9:8–17.

Jesus knew that the man's neighbors would be shocked at his drastic change. As word of the blind man's transformation quickly spread, someone took the Pharisees to go see the man. Maybe the neighbors wanted to share the miracle with the Pharisees, inviting them into wonder and joy. Or maybe the neighbors had heard the Pharisees were looking for reasons to condemn this radical teacher, and they wanted to score points with powerful religious leaders by bringing this to their attention.

6. In 9:14, we learn the reason some of the Pharisees used this miracle to build their case against Jesus. On what day did Jesus heal the blind man?

God designed the Sabbath as a day of rest and commanded that His people honor it. So religious leaders took God's beautiful and succinct provision and made an itemized list of thirty-nine forbidden classes of work, along with explanatory subcategories. Kneading was forbidden work, which included the mixing of dirt and saliva. At best, this was all a well-meaning attempt to clarify God's law in practical terms. But the problem was that the Pharisees put their clarifications on the same level as God's law. (It would be as if the speed limit were sixty miles per hour, and they insisted that everyone only go forty-five. In this scenario, they would punish anyone who drove forty-six miles per hour, even though God's law allowed for it.) They built a fence around God's law, and they called their fence the law.

7. Read Deuteronomy 4:2 and 12:32. What did God say about adding to His law?

God's law was already perfect, given for human flourishing; their additions to His perfect law were shortsighted at best, and selfish, controlling, and arrogant at worst.

8. *Review 9:18–23.*

As the Pharisees interrogated the blind man—let's call him the *seeing* man from now on—they doubted he was ever blind to begin with. So they asked his parents.

9. Why did the seeing man's parents send the Pharisees back to their son? What does this tell you about the Pharisees' motivation at that time?

As the Pharisees continued their unrelenting quest to silence Christ, it would become even more clear that what seemed a heresy to the spiritually blind was, without a doubt, eternal truth to those who could see. We'll pick up here tomorrow.

John 9:24–41

 READ JOHN 9:24–41

As we pick back up with the seeing man (formerly the blind man) today, take note that this all happened during the Feast of Tabernacles, also called the Feast of Booths. Light played a big role in this feast. Lampstands with candles lit the halls of the temple and the people read Old Testament Scriptures about light.

1. Read Isaiah 9:2 and write it below.

Light invites us to see, but some turn away, remaining in the dark instead.

2. Review 9:24–34.

The seeing man was interrogated again by the Pharisees. Despite all the questions they asked him, trying to figure out who Jesus was, they never got the answer they were looking for. Or so they thought. Their answer was the most obvious one all along: Jesus was exactly who He said He was.

In 9:24, the Pharisees told the seeing man to "give glory to God." With that phrase, they were asking him to swear a solemn oath and tell the truth, which of course, the man had already been doing. He didn't downplay or shrink away from the testimony of what Jesus had done for him, so he *was* giving glory to God!

3. Fill in the seeing man's glorious statement from 9:25.

"One thing I do know, _____ _____ _____ _____ _____, _____

_____ _____."

When the unrelenting Pharisees asked the man yet again what Jesus did and how He did it, the seeing man's exasperation might have led to a bit of sarcasm, because he asked them if *they* wanted to be Jesus's disciples. As the Pharisees recoiled, the seeing man used logic to preach a short sermon; he explained that only someone sent from God could do what Jesus had done.

Before the discovery of antibiotics, blindness was a tragically common result of severe infection. Sometimes people recovered from this type of blindness, and Jesus had healed a number of blind people. But before Jesus healed *this* man, no one who was born blind had ever been healed of their disability.

4. Keeping in mind the seeing man's testimony and the first-century understanding of the correlation between sin and sickness, explain why the Pharisees expelled the man from the synagogue in 9:34.

For what wasn't the first time, the Pharisees ignored the law they claimed to love so much by casting this man out without following the prescribed process. It seems their motive wasn't to cleanse their places of worship from blasphemy, but to protect their fragile egos.

5. Review 9:35–38. In 9:35, who sought out whom? What does that tell you about the heart of Jesus?

6. Review 9:39–41.

In John 5, when Jesus defended Himself against the religious leaders' accusations, He explained that God the Father entrusted righteous judgment to God the Son. Here, Jesus shared a sobering truth: Though they glimpse the light, some will remain in darkness. The Pharisees had heard Jesus teach; they'd listened as He explained theology; they'd talked to people He healed; and they'd seen Him change lives. And instead of coming into the light of belief, they stayed in the darkness and desperately tried to keep others in the dark with them.

But there were those—like the seeing man—who walked into His light. When Jesus gave the man his sight, there's no question that his life was changed. But the more he reflected on and recounted the story of what Jesus had done for him, the more his heart was transformed.

7. Review chapter 9 to fill in the table below.

Verse	What did the seeing man say about Jesus?
9:11	
9:17	
9:33	
9:38	(after Jesus calls Himself the Son of Man)

The seeing man's eyes were truly opened not when he was healed, but when he believed in Jesus. Even as his own community interrogated and rejected him, the light of Jesus shone all the brighter. When we reflect on what Jesus has done in our lives, His light shines brighter.

8. Reflect on something Jesus has done for you and write about it below. How has that helped you see more of His character?

Jesus is the light by which we see, and He's where the joy is!

9. What stood out to you most in this week's study? Why?

10. What did you learn or relearn about God and His character this week?

Corresponding
Psalm & Prayer

 READ PSALM 27

1. What correlation do you see between Psalm 27 and this week's study of Jesus as God?

2. What portions of this psalm stand out to you most?

3. Close by praying this prayer aloud:

Father,
    You are light, and You spoke light into being. It's only because of You that I see.

Like the blind man, I've known the darkness caused by a fallen world. And like David, I've also known the darkness caused by my own sin. I have lied. I have cheated. I have hated Your image bearers when I've mocked them. I have taken advantage of the vulnerable with my apathy and inaction. I confess my sin, and I repent from it.

Teach me Your way; lead me on Your path.

One day, I'll live in Your glorious light and gaze on Your beauty forever. Until then, as I wait, remind me that waiting isn't passive; it trusts and hopes and seeks. Teach me to seek light, no matter how dark life gets.

I surrender my life to You, Lord—every moment of my day, each decision I make, I yield my will and way to Your perfect will and way.

I love You too. Amen.

Rest, Catch Up, or Dig Deeper

 WEEKLY CHALLENGE

Light is an ongoing theme in John, and it's heavily featured in chapters 8 and 9. This week, set aside an early morning or late evening time for prayer. Leave your phone in a different space. Turn off the electric lights and light a candle instead or build a fire (be safe!). Notice that no matter how dark it gets around the candle or fire, the light is always there, fighting the darkness. Thank God for sending the light of the world to us, and ask Him to show you how to lead others to the light.

John 10–11

The Attentiveness of God

DAILY BIBLE READING

Day 1: John 10:1–21

Day 2: John 10:22–42

Day 3: John 11:1–27

Day 4: John 11:28–44

Day 5: John 11:45–57

Day 6: Psalm 23

Day 7: Catch-Up Day

Corresponds to Days 297 and 302 of *The Bible Recap*.

WEEKLY CHALLENGE

See page 129 for more information.

DAY 1

John 10:1–21

READ JOHN 10:1–21

1. Review 10:1–6.

After the dramatic interaction between the seeing man (formerly the blind man) and the Pharisees, Jesus warned the crowd about wicked religious leaders and emphasized His own good character. He used a relatable analogy: sheep and shepherds. In the Old Testament, religious leaders were called shepherds (Isaiah 56:11; Jeremiah 3:15), and people in this ancient culture were familiar with agrarian terminology.

2. Use a Bible study tool to describe a sheepfold. Include as much detail as possible.

Jesus warned the crowd that not everyone who interacted with the sheep had good intentions for the sheep. He used two distinct words—*thief* (*kleptēs*) and *robber* (*lēstēs*)—to show how one type tries to take the flock by trickery or deception and the other by violence or destruction. While wicked leaders are hopping fences, the shepherd enters the sheepfold the correct way and rightly tends to the flock.

3. Using 10:3–5 as your guide, match the action with the person. More than one action may apply.

Shepherd	tries (and fails) to lead the sheep, sheep flee from him
Sheep	calls his sheep by name, leads them out, brings out all his own, goes before the sheep
Stranger	hear the shepherd's voice, know the shepherd's voice, follow the shepherd

In the same way you may use a special voice when you talk to your pets, shepherds used a distinct call for their sheep. The animals knew the voice of the shepherd because of the time they'd spent together, and they willingly followed the shepherd because of the trust they'd built.

4. How can you recognize the voice of the Good Shepherd? Describe how you hear from Him and discern His prompting and calling to you.

5. Review 10:7–18.

Here, we see the third of Jesus's metaphorical *I am* statements in John's gospel: "I am the door of the sheep." When you studied the sheepfold, you likely read that the shepherd sits at the door (the opening) of the fold and guards the sheep at night. When Jesus announced that He was the door, He was telling them, *"I'm the* only *way in."*

This statement carries another meaning, which He reiterates in His fourth metaphorical *I am* statement: "I am the good shepherd." The shepherd is the one who lies down in the entry of the sheepfold. And He's not just their shepherd—He's *good* at being their shepherd. He protects them from those who seek to harm them or take advantage of them. Remember, He's talking to a crowd who just witnessed religious leaders get riled up because a wounded sheep was healed! Jesus was saying, *"The shepherds among you are wicked, but I'm the Good Shepherd prophesied in Ezekiel"* (Ezekiel 34:15, 23)! He invited them to enter His sheepfold to find protection and rest.

In churches today, some shepherds may knowingly (or unknowingly) cause harm to the sheep. When this happens, a natural reaction might be to flee the fold altogether. Jesus's identifying Himself as the Good Shepherd helps us to see that we can, instead, run to Him and trust His heart to rightly tend His sheep. We can rest in His ability to bring truth to light and to implement righteous justice, and we can rest in His plan to restore all things.

6. Use a Bible study tool to examine 10:16. Who are the sheep "not of this fold" that Jesus declares He will bring in? Why is this good news for many of us today?

7. Using 10:17–18 as your guide, fill in the table to indicate what the text reveals . . .

. . . about the relationship between the Father and the Son	
. . . about Jesus's authority	
. . . about Jesus's obedience to the Father	

8. Review 10:19–21.

As Jesus finished speaking, the Jews found themselves divided over their opinion of His teaching; they were divided about His identity. Some believed He was insane and demon-possessed. And others offered a rebuttal: "Can a demon open the eyes of the blind?"

The true Shepherd was standing in their midst, yet their eyes remained blind to see Him and their ears were deaf to His distinctive call.

John 10:22-42

 READ JOHN 10:22-42

1. Review 10:22–30.

In today's reading, the Jews were celebrating the Feast of Dedication (also known as Hanukkah), which takes place in the winter, around the time Christians celebrate Christmas. Winter is the rainy season in Israel, so it's possible they had some bad weather, because the text notes that Jesus was walking through the covered area of the temple's outer court.

2. Look up the word used for "gathered around" (10:24) and read all the other verses where this word is used in Scripture. There are five verses total. Look for a common theme among those verses. Who or what is generally being "gathered around" and by whom?

In almost every use of this word, the person or thing being gathered around is an enemy of those doing the "gathering around." It's much like how movies portray a group of playground bullies encircling their person of interest. In this scenario, Jesus was the person of interest, and the Jews surrounding Him made their request known: *"Stop keeping us in suspense and candidly tell us if you are the Christ!"*

Jesus had told them plainly, but they didn't believe. While He was careful how and when He shared His message, He had not kept His identity, His miracles, or His mission a secret.

3. Review the passages below and list how Jesus had made His identity known to the Jews.

Passage	Jesus's Revealed Identity
John 5:19–23	
John 7:28–29	
John 8:58	
John 10:9	
John 10:11	

Jesus explained to them that not only did His words bear witness about His deity, but His works did too. He wasn't just saying He was the Son of God; He was showing them. And repeatedly, they refused to listen and believe.

4. Fill in the blanks of Jesus's statement in 10:26.

"You do not _____ _____ you are ____ _____ ____ _____."

Jesus reiterated that His sheep hear His voice and are known by Him. He proclaimed the great gifts He gives to His sheep and restated the truth: No one—not a ravenous animal, not a greedy thief, not anyone—would snatch them out of His hand. His hand is strong and His heart is good, *and* His hand is doing the same work as His Father's hand.

5. In 10:29–30, what did Jesus declare about the Father's relationship with the sheep? With Jesus?

Jesus loves the sheep and tends the sheep as His Father does. Jesus and the Father are two distinct persons, and their oneness demonstrates their equality. Jesus is God just as the Father is God. Upon hearing this statement, the Jews were ready to stone Him.

6. **Review 10:31–42.**

Jesus refuted their attempt at stoning by responding with Scripture. He spoke to them—rabbi to rabbi—using Psalm 82 as the basis for His argument. Jesus reasoned along these lines: If those men, those earthly judges, were metaphorically called "gods" (Psalm 82:1, 6) because of their position, why would the Jews call it blasphemy when Jesus referred to Himself as the Son of God in light of all He had said and done?

7. In 10:37–38, what point was Jesus making to the Jewish leaders? How is your view of Jesus shaped by these words?

Jesus escaped their attempts to arrest Him and retreated to the place where JTB baptized Him. The people there remembered the words JTB had spoken about Jesus, and they realized those words had proven true—and many of them believed in Him.

8. Have you been impacted days, months, or years later by someone else's faithfulness to speak the truth of Jesus? Write a prayer of thanksgiving for those who have encouraged you with gospel truths!

John 11:1–27

 READ JOHN 11:1–27

1. Review 11:1–16.

Today's reading contains a jaw-dropping story that is found only in John's gospel. Lazarus was sick and desperately needed the kind of miracle Jesus had done for the masses. His family's close relationship with Jesus probably made it natural for his sisters to send an SOS to the miracle worker Himself, letting Him know Lazarus was sick. But Jesus didn't run immediately to their home, and He didn't speak a word to deliver a long-distance healing. Instead, He made a statement to the disciples that likely caused them to scratch their heads.

2. Fill in the blanks in 11:4 below.

"This illness does not _____ to _____. It is for the _____ of God, so that the _____ of _____ may be glorified _____ it."

Jesus knew what others didn't: Lazarus was going to die, but he wouldn't stay dead. Over the next two days, Jesus wasn't apathetically kicking rocks in the wilderness or wondering what to do next. His plan all along was to resurrect Lazarus, and His timing was specific. In their culture, a person had to be dead four days to be considered *truly* dead. Many scholars believe Jesus's delay was intentional, magnifying His miracle.

3. In 11:9–10, what does it mean to "walk in the day" and "walk in the night"? For additional help, see Matthew 4:16, John 1:4, John 8:12, and Hebrews 1:3.

Finally, Jesus began His walk toward Bethany, knowing that the great miracle He was about to perform would ruffle the feathers of the religious elite and that it would ultimately lead to His own death and resurrection. The disciples were concerned by His desire to walk back into angry-crowd country, but Thomas—more than just a doubter—was willing to die with Him.

4. Review 11:17–27.

When Jesus arrived at His friend's house, mourners were already there. Lazarus was, in fact, dead, and his sisters were heartbroken. Can you picture Martha's anguish as she said, "*Jesus if you had been here, this wouldn't have happened!*"? And yet, she immediately followed her words of grief by demonstrating great belief: "But even now, I know that whatever you ask from God, God will give you" (11:22). She was honest with her disappointment in His delay, but her sadness didn't erode her faith. She likely wasn't hoping for a miracle anymore, but she remained committed to trusting God.

Martha stood in the presence of God—the one powerful enough to resurrect her brother and the one whose own resurrection would redeem her—as He said to her, "I am the resurrection and the life." This was His fifth metaphorical *I am* statement, and it is the great hope for us all. And Jesus's words here are echoed repeatedly in the New Testament, reminding us that because of Him, we're saved out of death and into eternal life!

5. Fill in the table below with the belief and its result.

Verse	Belief	Result
John 3:16		
John 3:36		
John 12:46		
Romans 10:9		
Acts 16:31		

Through His own death, Jesus conquered death forever. Though Martha didn't yet understand what He was saying, Jesus was planting the seed for her to understand it retrospectively. Notice, He didn't follow up with "Do you understand?" He asked her, "Do you believe?" We aren't required to understand everything perfectly but to believe in Him regardless of whatever remains a mystery to us. For those wrestling through doubt or a lack of understanding, remember this: *He does the doing.* He gives us the ability to believe, and He grants more belief as we wrestle through our doubt.

6. What doubt or disappointment are you experiencing right now? How can you practically "walk in the day" with Jesus amid these feelings? Mark 9:24 is the honest cry of a man seeking help in a difficult situation. Write your own heart cry to God in the space below.

John 11:28–44

 READ JOHN 11:28–44

Because today's reading is the continuation of yesterday's conversation, some of our study will connect the two parts of this scene.

1. Review 11:28–37.

After Jesus's discussion with Martha, she told her sister Mary that "the Teacher" had arrived. It's interesting that she gave Jesus this title; in those days, rabbis weren't in the business of teaching women, but Jesus showed no partiality. Mary had indeed sat at His feet learning; He had indeed taught her (Luke 10:38–42). Upon hearing the news, Mary immediately went outside the village to meet with Jesus; the visitors—who were there to console her—followed, assuming she was going to visit the grave.

2. Revisit the sisters' interactions with Jesus in 11:20–35. Draw a check mark by Martha's words and actions and by Jesus's response to her. And draw a plus sign by Mary's words and actions and by Jesus's response to her.

Words:

"Lord, if you had been here, my brother would not have died."

"Lord, if you had been here, my brother would not have died."

Actions:

Went out immediately to meet Jesus.

Stayed in the house until Jesus called for her, then fell at His feet.

Jesus's Response:

"Your brother will rise again. . . . Everyone who lives and believes in me shall never die. Do you believe this?"

He asked where Lazarus had been placed, then He wept.

These two sisters made the same statement to Jesus, but the statement was couched in two different sets of actions and tones. It might be easy to categorize Martha as the logical "thinker" who takes practical action and Mary as the "feeler" who leans into her devotion and emotion. But Jesus didn't claim that one disposition was better than the other. Instead, He adapted His response to suit the needs of each person. With Martha, He met her in her logic, and He reasoned with her about His plan for resurrection. With Mary, He met her in her emotion, and He wept.

3. Use a Greek lexicon to define *weeping* (11:33) and *wept* (11:35). How do these two words differ?

"Jesus wept." This is the shortest verse in the entire Bible, but it's no less weighty than any other. This verse reveals that God in the flesh—the God in whose likeness we're made—has emotions. There's no sin or shame in our tears. And as we read about His tears, we see that He truly is a man acquainted with grief (Isaiah 53:3); He understands our suffering and sympathizes with us (Hebrews 4:15).

4. Think of a time when you were overcome with sadness. Is your tendency to run *from* God as if He doesn't understand or to draw *near*, knowing that He cares? If it's the former, how does this text change your view of God's heart toward you?

As the crowd saw Him weeping, they observed, *"Wow, Jesus really loved him."* Some added, *"I wonder why He couldn't save him?"* While some think these are genuine words of sympathy, others believe this was a jab at Jesus's power or motives—perhaps the crowd held a wide range of opinions. Jesus, committed to His plan and not thwarted by the opinions of man, was about to stun them with what happened next.

5. Review 11:38–44.

Jesus arrived at the tomb with a mission. And this is the second time in only a few verses that Scripture says He was "deeply moved."

6. Look up the phrase *deeply moved* (11:33, 11:38) in a Greek lexicon and note what you find. Now look up the phrase *greatly troubled* in a Greek lexicon (11:33) and note what you find. What do you think prompted Jesus to feel this way?

The word for "deeply moved" carries the tone of anger, not of grief. Some scholars believe He was angry at those who disbelieved, but it seems more likely that He was angry at death itself, especially since this emotion is first mentioned during His conversation with Mary.

Graveside, Jesus instructed the stone to be removed. Notice how the practical Martha gently reminded Him, *"He's been in there for four days, Jesus; he's going to stink."* Jesus responded to her by reminding her of their previous conversation.

7. Fill in the blanks from 11:40 below.

"Did I not tell you that if you _____ you would _____ the _____ of God?"

Jesus didn't publicly shame Martha for "being Martha"; instead, He gently reminded her to put her belief into action. He didn't need her faith—or her sister's faith—to do the miracle. He could accomplish His plan without them. He knew they would see the result and be happy, but without truly believing, they'd miss out on seeing the glory of God.

8. In 11:41–42, Who did Jesus address in prayer? Why did He pray aloud in this way? What was He hoping to accomplish?

After He publicly prayed, knowing He'd conquer death, Jesus spoke to Lazarus as if he was already alive, "Lazarus! Come out!" And the man came out from where he was buried—graveclothes and all! Lazarus was fully alive, but still dressed head-to-toe like a dead man. (In fact, he probably had to *hop* out of the grave because of how tightly bound dead bodies were!) Then, Jesus commanded the community around him to untie his burial garments. Lazarus had been miraculously raised from the dead, but Jesus still invited those around him to participate in the process. How beautiful that perhaps *even those who doubted* got to participate in the joy and awe of his healing!

John 11:45–57

 READ JOHN 11:45-57

1. Review 11:45–54.

Remember what took place in yesterday's reading? A man, wrapped in burial clothes, who'd been lying in a grave for *four* days, stood up and walked out of his grave—fully alive! Calling this a big miracle is an understatement, but notice John didn't stop to play a highlight reel of what happened next in Lazarus's life. Instead, the author kept the main thing the main thing: proclaiming Jesus as God. The witnesses of this miracle had two very different reactions: One group believed, while the other ran away to report Jesus to the Jewish religious authorities.

2. Use a Bible study tool to match the religious title with the description.

Pharisees	from the tribe of Levi; a high position among the Israelites
Council	the intercessor between God and His people; in charge of temple/tabernacle worship
High priest	Sanhedrin; a political and judicial council headed by the high priest
Chief priests	experts of the law; believed in the resurrection and followed strict legal traditions not listed in the Torah

3. Who was the high priest at the time?

Keeping up with religious titles and their meanings can be tricky, but it's not impossible. A little extra reading in your favorite Bible commentary will equip you in no time! Don't rush through without trying to better understand these details, because they will help you tremendously in the days ahead.

4. What complaint did the religious elite have against Jesus in 11:47? What fears did they mention in 11:48?

Caiaphas gave an aggressive response to the men around him and presented a logical—albeit outrageously immoral—solution: *"It's better for one man to die so that our nation and our place of worship will last forever."* He didn't realize it, but he'd spoken a prophetic statement. The high priest shared God's plan with others and was totally unaware.

And as John captured the story, he used this moment to highlight a deeper meaning: Jesus would die to save many from perishing.

5. How do Jesus's words in John 3:16 complement Caiaphas's words in 11:50?

6. Summarize 11:51–52 in your own words. What does it mean to "gather into one [nation] the children who are scattered abroad"? (See John 10:16 and/or a Bible study tool for help.)

The religious elite plotted Jesus's death to preserve their religious order, but God's plan was not interrupted by their wicked schemes. In fact, He even used the sinful motives of man to accomplish His great purposes.

After this, Jesus stopped walking openly among the Jews, not because He was afraid of them, but because He knew His time had not yet come (see John 7:30). He and His disciples went to stay in the desert village of Ephraim for the time being. The location of the town is uncertain, but some maps place it roughly five miles north of Jerusalem.

7. Review 11:55–57.

This is the third and final Passover mentioned in John, and Jesus was certainly the talk of the town at this feast as people gathered and began their preparations. As yeast (leaven) was removed from homes, ritual washings were taking place, and unblemished animals were acquired, the Lamb of God—who would take away the sins of the world—waited outside the city. And our reading leaves us with a cliffhanger as the festal preparations begin.

The true Passover Lamb remained willing to endure all that was before Him, and He stayed in submission to the Father's plan, established from before the beginning (Revelation 13:8). And even knowing all He would endure, He was joyfully committed to the plan (Hebrews 12:2). He waited, and now we wait. He submitted, and now we can submit. He expected joy, and now we can expect joy too—because He's where the joy is!

8. What stood out to you most in this week's study? Why?

9. What did you learn or relearn about God and His character this week?

Corresponding Psalm & Prayer

 READ PSALM 23

1. What correlation do you see between Psalm 23 and this week's study of Jesus as God?

2. What portions of this psalm stand out to you most?

3. Close by praying this prayer aloud:

Father,
You are the Good Shepherd. You invite me into Your fold, and there You give me rest. You care for the flock, and You care for each sheep. Your love is vast, extending around the entire world. And

Your love is personal, caring for me in every moment, through every emotion.

I know how good it is to walk with You in the day, but I've sometimes chosen to walk in the night. And so I've stumbled. I've become consumed by unruly emotions, instead of allowing them to point me to You. I've directed my anger at You instead of humbly bringing it to You. I've been lost in my fear instead of asking You to guide me through it. I've even given myself credit for my joy, instead of praising You for it.

Let my emotions be guideposts that point me to You. Like Mary, let me mourn with You, the one acquainted with grief. Like Martha, let sorrow be a catalyst to deeper belief. Because You are good, no matter where You lead me, I know that all will be well, and all manner of things will be made well.

I surrender my life to You, Lord—every moment of my day, each decision I make, I yield my will and way to Your perfect will and way.

I love You too. Amen.

Rest, Catch Up, or Dig Deeper

 WEEKLY CHALLENGE

In Day 2, we read that JTB's testimony of Jesus continued to impact people in such a way that once Jesus arrived, they marveled and believed. His words and actions laid the groundwork for people to believe, and they made a lasting impact. You likely have a person in your life who made a lasting impact on you as well. Write a note of gratitude and encouragement to that person and share it with them.

John 12–13

The Servant Heart of God

DAILY BIBLE READING

Day 1: John 12:1–19

Day 2: John 12:20–36a

Day 3: John 12:36b–50

Day 4: John 13:1–20

Day 5: John 13:21–38

Day 6: Psalm 113

Day 7: Catch-Up Day

Corresponds to Days 307 and 314 of *The Bible Recap.*

WEEKLY CHALLENGE

See page 155 for more information.

John 12:1–19

 READ JOHN 12:1–19

In today's reading, it's six days before Passover—the last week before Jesus's death. Nearly half of John's gospel is devoted to this week of Jesus's life.

1. Review 12:1–8.

In Bethany of Judea, a small village just outside the city walls of Jerusalem, Lazarus's family threw a dinner party in Jesus's honor. This dinner was likely given in honor of Jesus's raising Lazarus from the dead. So imagine the irony of celebrating Lazarus's return to life even as Jesus was being anointed for His death.

2. Match the party attendees with their actions in 12:2–6.

Martha	expressing frustration with Mary's actions
Lazarus	anointing Jesus's feet with expensive nard
Jesus	serving
Mary	reclining at the table
Judas	reclining at the table with Jesus

Outside the walls of the house, there was a verbal warrant floating around for Jesus's arrest. But inside the walls, Jesus was being celebrated and honored in ways that escape our modern understanding. This perfumed nard, which scholars say was probably from the Himalayas, was worth roughly a year's wages. Either this family was very rich or—more likely—it was the most valuable thing they owned. As Mary anointed Him, the house was filled with the fragrance of the perfume. But perhaps not everyone there found it fragrant.

3. Which of the following is true of the aroma in 2 Corinthians 2:14–17 (use the NLT):

   A. It is perceived differently by those who are being saved and by those who are perishing.

   B. It is perceived similarly by all.

   C. To those who are perishing, it is a dreadful smell of death and doom.

   D. To those who are being saved, it is a life-giving perfume.

   E. A, C, and D

   F. All of the above

While Judas's statement may seem thoughtful, discerning, and practical, John revealed that Judas's motives had more to do with the fact that he'd been using the money bag as his personal piggy bank. Judas's hypocrisy would soon be revealed.

4. Are there areas of your life where you might have ulterior motives hiding behind claims of practicality? If so, what are they? Pray Psalm 139:23–24 over each of these areas.

If we look at 12:8 out of context, we might be worried that Jesus was being callous about the poor in His response to Judas. But He was actually referencing Deuteronomy 15:10–11, which covers laws about caring for the poor. Jesus's heart for the poor was both gentle and active. And in this scenario, it was fitting for Mary to anoint Him for His death—He knew it was rapidly approaching.

5. Review 12:9–11.

Many people were drawn to Jesus because of the resurrection of Lazarus. But again, we see that Jesus had a polarizing impact on His audience. There were some who wanted to kill Lazarus because Jesus had raised him from the dead. How ironic! But we also see that many turned to believe in Jesus because of it. When we encounter the truth, we're forced to pick sides—we cannot be faced with the deity of Jesus and remain neutral.

6. Review 12:12–19.

As the Jews gathered in Jerusalem to celebrate Passover, they heard that Jesus was in town—this resurrector, this miracle worker, who was upsetting the people in power. *Surely this is the Messiah, the one to overthrow Rome?* There were likely zealots among the crowd, men who had trained as assassins to stage their revolt against Rome when the time came. They awaited a leader worth following into that political rebellion.

In first-century Israel, the palm branch was used by the zealots as a militaristic sign of revolution. It represented independence and victory. As their hope for freedom approached, they gathered palm branches to honor Him. "Hosanna!" they cried. The word means "Save us!" But they weren't seeking salvation from their sins; they had no lens for understanding that the God of the universe was inviting them into an *eternal* kind of salvation and freedom. They were shortsighted, focusing only on the temporary.

So imagine their surprise when, instead of entering on a war horse like the military power they'd surely imagined, Jesus entered on a donkey. He subverted their expectations while also fulfilling Zechariah's prophecy from five hundred years earlier (Zechariah 9:9). These were things His disciples would understand only in retrospect.

7. Look up Revelation 7:9–10 and fill in the blanks from 7:9 below.

". . . a great multitude that no one could number, from every _____,

from all _____ and _____ and _____ . . ."

Today, we await the fulfillment of that prophecy. But this time, it will be every nation, tribe, people, and language waving palm branches before the Lamb. The only way every nation, tribe, and people can raise the symbol of victory is if we are all united under one God and King. Palm Sunday set the stage for that great *someday* when the whole world will go after Him.

DAY 2

John 12:20–36a

 READ JOHN 12:20–36A

Yesterday's reading ended with Jesus's triumphal entry. The Pharisees responded, *"Look how the whole world has gone after Him."* They were likely being hyperbolic, speaking out of their irritation with Jesus's popularity. But as we've seen happen before in the book of John, the Pharisees were being unintentionally prophetic—because that's exactly what happened next. Today we pick up with other people groups besides the Jews seeking Jesus out.

1. Review 12:20–26.

The Greeks approached Philip first, likely because he was the disciple with a Greek name. We aren't told their background, so they may have been converts to Judaism, or perhaps they just possessed the same curiosity the Greeks were known for.

Philip and Andrew told Jesus that the Greeks wanted to meet with Him, but in typical Jesus fashion, He didn't seem to answer the question He was asked. Instead, He began talking about how He had to stay the course. It's unclear whether Jesus met with the Greeks, but given His message, it seems, perhaps, that He shared these words with only His disciples and the immediate crowd.

Many people—the zealots, the Pharisees, now the Greeks—had been seeking Jesus and for various reasons, but Jesus pointed out that in His humanity, He was unable to meet with all the people who sought Him. However, He knew there was one way for a single seed to bear much fruit: It must die. The only way He could serve the multitudes who needed Him was through His death.

2. Write 12:25 in your own words.

3. What aspects of your life feel most challenging to "hate" or view as less valuable than following Jesus?

Jesus's teaching on hating one's life wasn't a call to depression or a negative outlook. Instead, He was pointing out that we should be willing to put anything in our lives on the chopping block that competes with our allegiance to Him. Following Him is where true blessing and favor lies. And even as He prophesied His own death, Jesus knew it wasn't the end. He invited followers to be near Him, to serve, to receive honor from the Father.

4. Review 12:27–36a.

Though Jesus was troubled by the plan for His death, He was prepared for it and committed to it. He knew it was His purpose. As He talked with the Father about it, the Father responded audibly so that even those in the crowd could hear—and in fact, that was God's intent, that the onlookers might witness this unity of the Father and Son, affirming the plan.

5. Look up Jesus's use of "lifted up" in 12:32 in a Greek lexicon. Write all the meanings you find.

As Jesus continued talking about His death, the crowd expressed their confusion. They thought the Messiah would never leave. "Son of Man" is a messianic title Jews would've recognized from Daniel's prophecy. We saw mention of this in our study of John 3:14–15, where Jesus told Nicodemus the Son of Man must be lifted up just as Moses lifted up the serpent in the wilderness.

6. Look up Daniel 7:13–14. Which is not true of the Son of Man?

    A. He came with the clouds of heaven

    B. He was given dominion, glory, and a kingdom

    C. All peoples would serve Him

    D. His dominion would not pass away

    E. His kingdom would be destroyed

It seems this crowd was sincere in their questions, truly trying to understand who He was. Perhaps they had been convinced by what had just happened—the voice of God booming through the atmosphere like thunder, undeniable. As they asked questions, Jesus met them with the offer of repentance and belief—to turn from the darkness and walk in His light.

John 12:36b–50

 READ JOHN 12:36B-50

1. Review 12:36b–43.

Up to this point in John, we've witnessed a bounty of signs and miracles performed by Jesus during His ministry.

2. Write down a few you recall from our study so far.

They saw the reality of His power but failed to believe in the divinity those signs served to highlight. Having done all He could, He finally hid from them. John said this served an important purpose—fulfilling Isaiah's prophecy.

3. Using your favorite Bible study tools (a commentary, study Bible, etc.), do some research on 12:40 and write down what you find.

This passage tells us Isaiah said these things because he saw God's glory and it motivated him to action.

4. **Look up** *glory* **(12:41) in a Greek lexicon.** Describe it below in your own words.

5. Is this definition of *glory* different from what you thought it meant? If so, how?

How sobering to consider the places where we, like the authorities in today's reading, are prone to love the cheap glory of man more than the better glory that comes from the almighty God.

6. Fill out the table below with a few examples.

What you tend to get praise for from people	What you tend to *seek* praise for from people

A lot of the things we're praised for by people are gifts from God. But do we know in our hearts that the glory of God is better than any praise we could ever receive from humankind?

7. Pray the truth of Galatians 1:10 over your desires and motivations.

8. Review John 12:44–50.

In John's gospel account, these words are the last speech Jesus gave to the public before His arrest. These words seem to serve as His final and authoritative clarification on much of what He had already told the public about Himself.

9. Draw lines to complete Jesus's statements in 12:44–46.

"Whoever believes in me, believes . . ."

"light."

"And whoever sees me sees"

"in him who sent me."

"I have come into the world as"

"him who sent me."

Jesus's declaration that He came into the world as light points to the fulfillment of another prophecy from Isaiah. Within this promise of light, there's also the implication that those who don't believe remain in darkness. He came via the Father's authority to save a world that needed saving.

10. In 12:47–48, Jesus makes an important distinction. Fill in the blanks:

"I did not come to _____ the world but to _____ the world."

You may remember from our study of John 5:22 that Jesus said, "The Father judges no one, but has entrusted all judgment to the Son." It may *appear* that Scripture is contradicting itself here. *Is Jesus the judge or not?* We'll dig deeper into that question and the roles within the Trinity in our study of John 14. But what's important to note here is, in 12:47, Jesus wasn't actually addressing whether He's the judge—He was saying that's not the *reason He came.*

John 13:1–20

 READ JOHN 13:1–20

1. *Review 13:1–11.*

The hour had come. John tells us Jesus loved His own to the end. And out of His love, He washed their feet, a job that customarily fell to the lowest person in the household. Even with a devil-incited betrayer among them, the God of the universe took the position of a servant—out of His great love.

2. Why do you think John included 13:3 *before* Jesus began to wash? How do Jesus's foreknowledge and His understanding of His identity as God equip Him for this role?

At first, Peter didn't want Jesus to wash his feet. But once Jesus clarified the importance of it, Peter told Jesus to wash all of him. This brings up an interesting element of our faith.

3. Complete Jesus's response to Peter in 13:10: "The one who has bathed . . ."

    A. ". . . does need to wash, except for his feet, but is not completely clean."

    B. ". . . does need to wash, except for his feet."

    C. ". . . does not need to wash, but is not completely clean."

    D. ". . . does not need to wash, except for his feet, but is completely clean."

4. What do you think Jesus meant by this?

Jesus was making an important distinction for us here between sanctification and justification.

5. In a Bible dictionary, look up the words *justification* and *sanctification*, and write the definitions below in your own words.

    Justification:

    Sanctification:

Once we belong to God, He declares us clean. This is justification—the legal term Scripture uses to indicate our being declared righteous because Jesus has cleansed us from the consequences of our sins and granted His righteousness to us. Because of His finished work on the cross, we are adopted into God's family, made saints as His sons and daughters—once and for all time.

And yet, we are still sinners. We live in the reality of our daily sin. Every time we go out into the world, the dust of the world sticks to us—or, as in this analogy, *our feet still get dirty*. This is why we need God's ongoing work of sanctification to continue to grow and purify us, conforming us to the image of Christ. As long as we live in these bodies of flesh, we are saints with dirty feet—saved and persevering.

6. Review 13:12–20.

After living out this example of service for His disciples, He asked if they understood what it all meant. We can assume they probably didn't, because He went on to explain it to them. He said He was giving them an example to follow, telling them to become servants of each other.

This can be a hard message to swallow. We might willingly and joyfully wash the feet of Jesus. But He said to wash one another's feet. And He didn't qualify His instructions—He didn't say to wash only the feet of people you think deserve it or the people who don't annoy you. Jesus washed the feet of Judas, who would betray Him unto death in mere hours.

And He said, "A servant is not greater than his master" in conjunction with washing their feet—but that example would pale in comparison to the greater service Jesus was about to offer them all through His death. Jesus entered into a wide array of service to His people.

7. Can you think of a specific time when you said no to a role or task or complained about it, because it felt too menial or lowly? If so, describe the situation. If you had the opportunity to rewrite that story, how would Jesus's humbling example adjust your approach?

8. Look up the meaning of *blessed* (13:17) in a lexicon or Bible dictionary. Write what you find.

Blessing is promised for those who serve! This helpful reminder can serve as a joyful invitation when we're tempted to deny service opportunities. Jesus didn't have to serve Judas, but He washed his feet anyway. And yet, Jesus reiterated that the betrayer was among them and would soon be revealed. He did this not to "out" Judas but to supply another bit of evidence that this was all part of the plan leading up to His messianic triumph.

The last nine words of 13:20 might've reminded you of what He said in 12:44 from yesterday's reading.

9. Read both passages and fill in the blanks.

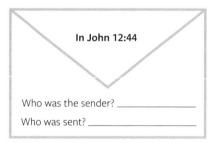
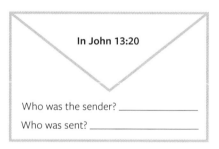

Just as Mary washed Jesus's feet to prepare Him for the work He must do, Jesus washed His disciples' feet here in preparation for the work they would do after Him. And just as Jesus explained that He was sent by the Father, He reminded them that it would soon be their turn. And they would go with the authority of the one who sent Him. We do not go alone into our mission to share the gospel and serve the church—we go with the authority and blessing of the Father!

10. Fill in the blanks from Romans 11:36.

For ____ _____ and _____ _____ and ____ _____ are _____ _____.

To Him be glory forever. Amen.

John 13:21–38

 READ JOHN 13:21-38

Today's reading picks up right where we left off yesterday: same location, same scene. In fact, the handful of chapters that follow all seem to take place in this room. Together, they're often called the Upper Room Discourse (especially chapters 14–17). This block of Jesus's teaching is found only in John's gospel, giving us His last words to His disciples before He was arrested later that night.

1. Review 13:21–30.

In John, we've seen that Jesus knew how this would all play out; He knew He would rise again after He died. Yet in 13:21, He still grieved when He reiterated His impending betrayal, even knowing His death would end in joy.

2. Does this surprise you? Why or why not?

In modern faith culture, people can be quick to throw out verses like Romans 8:28, putting a Band-Aid over grief: "All things work together for good, for those who are called according to his purpose." But this moment in the upper room (and many others in Jesus's life) reminds us that His knowing everything would work out for good didn't stop Him from feeling the pain of the moment. Scripture regularly mentions God's heart being grieved.

3. How does Isaiah 53:3 describe Jesus? Circle all that apply.

    A. Despised and rejected

    B. Always cheerful, no matter the circumstance

    C. A man of sorrows

    D. A man of few words

    E. Acquainted with grief

    F. A man so strong He couldn't be moved

God meets us and ministers to us in our affliction—and He grieves with us, even when He knows the end is good.

4. Using 13:22–29 as your guide, complete the following table:

Who reclined at Jesus's side in verse 23?	
Who motioned to Him in verse 24?	
What did that disciple ask Jesus in verse 25?	
Who took the morsel in verse 26?	
What did Jesus say to him in verse 27?	
According to verse 28, who knew why He said it to him?	

If you're surprised no one realized that Judas had just been identified as the traitor, you're not alone. This is another pertinent example of non-Scriptural, cultural influences getting in the way of our understanding. You may have been picturing a table like the one in Leonardo da Vinci's painting *Last Supper*.

But tradition included a type of seating arrangement called *haseiba*—to recline on one's left side while performing many of the Seder rituals. So the table configuration would've actually looked more like the image below. We don't know exactly where each disciple was sitting, but we do know where some were seated.

5. In the image below, label the people whose locations around the table *are* mentioned in Scripture.

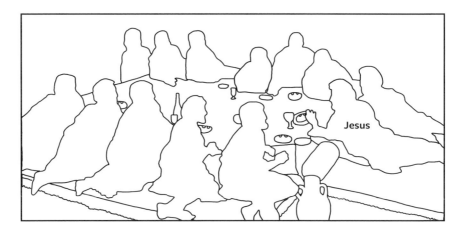

6. Compare 13:2 with 13:27. How are these two details about Judas different?

Jesus demonstrated His full humanity *and* His full deity in His words to Judas in 13:27. He seemed to fully understand what was happening in the spiritual realm, but He told Judas to not waste any time. Jesus didn't want to prolong the anticipation or the pain. Like many of us, it seems He wanted to get the hard part over with. Judas stepped into full traitorhood, and Jesus watched him leave the room to do it. Then Jesus had the poise to keep preaching. He gave them a "new" commandment.

7. Review 13:31–35. Look up 13:34's use of *new* in a Bible commentary. Write what you find.

Jesus knew that they were about to spend the rest of their lives experiencing persecution and death threats like they'd never seen. They were about to live through three days of immense grief. People with shared losses can grieve together, but sometimes they're also tempted to grieve *at* each other.

8. Have you been through a season of grief in which you saw this at play? If so, describe.

Jesus told them, *"This is how people will know you're My disciples: that you love one another."* It's the hardest thing, isn't it? It still is for us as disciples today. And Satan knows this. Can you imagine anything more harmful to the message of Christ than the disciples splintering and fighting each other?

9. A lack of love causes us to be less effective in many areas. List four of the ways mentioned in 1 Corinthians 13:1–3.

    A.

    B.

    C.

    D.

10. Review John 13:36–38.

Imagine the emotions in the final moment of today's passage. After Jesus saw Judas leave to betray Him, He told Peter that before morning, he'd also deny Him. Even Peter. But hold on to that heartbreak. As we follow Peter's story, we'll come to see that when we walk with Jesus, our biggest failings can become our mightiest callings.

All is not lost when we fail. Like Judas, Peter was a traitor, but we'll see him repent. There is hope for all of us sinners with dirty feet. Because Jesus is where the sanctification is, and He's where the joy is!

11. What stood out to you most in this week's study? Why?

12. What did you learn or relearn about God and His character this week?

Corresponding
Psalm & Prayer

 READ PSALM 113

1. What correlation do you see between Psalm 113 and this week's study of Jesus as God?

2. What portions of this psalm stand out to you most?

3. Close by praying this prayer aloud:

Father,

The psalmist asked, Who is like You? And we answer with him: No one! Your glory stretches beyond the heavens, yet You look down on the needy and raise us up. You make us part of Your family, Your royal family. From sunrise to sunset, and all through the night, let me join the chorus of sinners and saints around the world, singing, "Blessed be the name of the Lord!"

I rejoice that You make me a saint. And I acknowledge that—until You come again—I am still a sinner. Like Judas, I have been selfish with my belongings when they weren't even mine to begin with. Like the authorities scared of the Pharisees, I have sought man's cheap praise over God's eternal glory. Like Peter, I've seen signs and wonders, but my belief has been shaky, and I've sought to say magic words that will guarantee my salvation instead of growing in a steady and humble faith.

Lord, I believe. Help my unbelief. Teach me to become Your servant. Teach me to wash feet. Teach me to love like You love.

From You and through You and to You are all things. I put my trust in the one who holds it all.

I surrender my life to You, Lord—every moment of my day, each decision I make, I yield my will and way to Your perfect will and way.

I love You too. Amen.

Rest, Catch Up, or Dig Deeper

 WEEKLY CHALLENGE

On Day 4, we read about Jesus displaying the servant heart of God by washing the disciples' feet. This week, follow Jesus's example by planning an act of service for someone. Maybe it's cooking dinner, maybe it's meeting a need that's specific to them and makes them feel seen and known. Put some preparation and forethought into it, praying for them as you do.

┌─ Scripture to Memorize ─┐

If you abide in me, and my
words abide in you, ask
whatever you wish, and
it will be done for you.

John 15:7

John 14–15
The Triune Nature of God

DAILY BIBLE READING

Day 1: John 14:1–14
Day 2: John 14:15–24
Day 3: John 14:25–31
Day 4: John 15:1–17
Day 5: John 15:18–27
Day 6: Psalm 91
Day 7: Catch-Up Day

Corresponds to Day 315 of *The Bible Recap*.

WEEKLY CHALLENGE

See page 180 for more information.

John 14:1–14

 READ JOHN 14:1–14

1. Review 14:1–4.

"Do not be troubled" seems a difficult imperative in light of what Jesus told the disciples in chapter thirteen. But He gave them something better to cling to: belief. Their belief wasn't in an impersonal god—it was in the one they'd shared life with for three years. These men had a front-row seat and deep relationship with their God, who was wrapped in human flesh and living with them.

Before He made His journey to the cross, He spent time revealing truth that the disciples wouldn't fully understand until after His resurrection. He started by telling them what would be waiting for them when they finally got to where He was going.

2. Look back at 13:33 and 13:36. Why do you think the disciples were confused by Jesus's words in 14:3–4?

3. **Review 14:5–7.**

We've given Thomas the reputation of a doubter (something Jesus never said of him), but perhaps he simply felt safe enough to express when he didn't understand something. Moving forward, let's try to think of him as Honest Thomas. All twelve of the disciples were probably confused by Jesus's words, but Thomas was the first to voice it. Had Honest Thomas not asked, we wouldn't have the significant truth of John 14:6 and Jesus's sixth metaphorical *I am* statement.

4. **Look up 14:6 in a Bible commentary.** What aspects of this verse strike you as most profound?

Rather than chide Thomas for his misunderstanding, Jesus reiterated that even though the disciples had been with Him, they didn't yet fully understand. He wanted them to know that He and the Father were one, and that to know Jesus was to know and see the Father.

5. **Review 14:7b–11.** Why do you think Philip didn't get what he asked for?

After Jesus pushed back against Philip's request, He told them again to believe what He was telling them. He even conceded that if they needed more than His word, they should at least take His miracles into consideration. We tend to think that if our desire is a "good" one, God should give us what we want, how we want it, and when we want it. But God knows everything, including what we need! We can trust that His no is the kindest possible answer.

6. Has God ever revealed Himself to you or answered a prayer in a way that you weren't expecting or asking for? Was the result better or worse than what you'd hoped for? Briefly describe.

7. Review 14:12–14.

Jesus wanted the disciples to know that when He left, the work was far from over. He knew they would be discouraged and ready to quit. But they would continue in power, and their numbers would grow as the church was established! The "greater works" Jesus referred to in 14:12 are about *quantity*, not *quality*. Jesus spent three years doing earthly ministry, but the millions (or more) in the church would continue to minister to the world for thousands of years.

8. How might 14:13–14 be misunderstood apart from its context?

It will be helpful to remember that John 13–17 includes one long conversation—the Upper Room Discourse. Each day's reading will break Jesus's words in this scene into smaller pieces. So if today's reading feels like it ends with a cliffhanger, hold on to your hat! Tomorrow, Jesus will be giving the disciples a crash course on the Holy Spirit.

John 14:15–24

 READ JOHN 14:15–24

1. **Review 14:15–17.**

Anytime Scripture repeats itself—and perhaps especially when Jesus repeats Himself—it should catch our attention. In today's ten verses, Jesus said three times that if His disciples loved Him, they would keep His commands.

2. **Do a web search for the commands of Jesus in the Gospels.** Write down at least five of them, along with their chapter-verse references. Circle the one from your list that is the most difficult for you to obey.

Notice in 14:15 what Jesus said was the motivation for keeping His commands. It wasn't moral obligation, fear, pride, or striving for favor or blessing—it was love for Him. It's often easier to be motivated by our application points, our to-do list, or the praise of others. In fact, it's one of the persistent struggles Christians have experienced since the origin of the church.

3. Look up Revelation 2:2–5a and fill in the table below. Then note how love for Jesus might help you live out the command you circled above.

What did the church in Ephesus . . .

. . . get right?	
. . . get wrong?	
. . . need to do in response?	

Some of us have walked with Christ for so long that while we continue to do work in the name of Jesus, we've lost sight of our love for Him. We've become comfortable with a spiritual routine, rather than obeying out of a response to His love. We wonder why it's difficult to talk about Jesus with others, but the truth is that we talk about the things we love. If He's not part of your regular conversations, it might be worth taking inventory—not out of shame, but out of hope for *more joy* than you're currently experiencing. If that's you, take the prompt given to the disciples in the upper room and to the church at Ephesus: Remember why you love Jesus, repent of anything keeping you from Him, and get back to the basics.

Being told to believe over and over and then being told to obey out of love feels like a bigger command than broken and fallen humans can follow on their own. *And it is.* But the good news is that the disciples didn't have to accomplish belief or obedience on their own. Jesus said

He would ask the Father to give them another Helper to be with them forever!

4. **Use Bible study tools to circle the correct answers from 14:16.**

True or False: *Another* means something completely different.

The word *Helper* in the Greek (*paraklētos*) means: (circle all that apply)

- Counselor
- Advocate
- Tool for shaping clay
- Mediator
- Intercessor
- Bird native to Egypt

Up to this point, Jesus had told the disciples that they had seen the Father because they had been with Jesus. Here, He clued them in on the third member of the Trinity: the Spirit of truth. And—great news—they already knew Him personally because they'd been with Jesus and He was united with Jesus!

5. **Review 14:18–24.**

Jesus was leaving, but He wasn't leaving His disciples alone; He would come to them. He would fulfill this promise in three unique ways: His resurrection (John 20), the coming of His Spirit (Acts 2:1–4), and His future return in the last days (Revelation 22:12). Jesus would physically leave them for now, but that would be a good thing! It set the stage for His resurrection, which made eternal life possible for His disciples and everyone else who would believe in Him.

6. What assurance did Jesus give in 14:20? How would it help the disciples carry out the instructions of 14:21a?

Obedience motivated by love for God goes far beyond a one-sided human love.

7. In 14:21b, Jesus assured His disciples that those who love Him would be loved by the Father and Jesus and that He would _____ Himself to them (through the Holy Spirit).

How do each of these translations fill that blank?

ESV:

NIV:

CSB:

MSG:

In 14:22, John makes a clarifying statement about a disciple named Judas. Many of the disciples had more than one name (e.g., Simon/Peter, Matthew/Levi). Because John wrote his gospel several decades after the death of Jesus, it was important to him that readers not confuse the sincere Judas with Judas Iscariot. Though there are a few theories as to which disciple also had the moniker Judas, it seems that this is the same man referred to as Thaddaeus (in Mark's and Matthew's gospels).

The question Judas/Thaddaeus asked was a fair one. How was Jesus going to make Himself plain to them if He was leaving them? If we're honest, we may also feel confused about the concept of the Trinity. It's both simple and deeply complex—much like God Himself.

8. Review 14:23–24 and read 1 John 4:7–10. How do these verses help you better understand how the Triune God works within Himself and within us? Use Bible study tools if you need help.

Each person of the triune God plays a unique role in our salvation, but they are all united in their character, will, and plan. Though we'll never fully understand the Trinity on this side of eternity, we can understand it *more*. And that increased knowledge is what will drive our love and obedience!

John 14:25–31

 READ JOHN 14:25–31

1. Review 14:25–27.

Put yourself in the sandals of the disciples and how challenging it must've felt to follow Jesus as He explained what was about to happen:

- He made bold claims about His unity with the Father.
- He *kept* saying He would be leaving.
- He said you (somehow?) knew where He would be going.
- He said you couldn't go with Him.
- He said not to be scared because He would come back.
- He said He would send Someone to help you until He returned.

Despite their obvious confusion, Jesus continued explaining how things would go when He left. He knew the disciples wouldn't be able to understand without the Holy Spirit's help. They had no idea when this "Helper" would arrive.

2. Circle each member of the Trinity every time they show up (nouns, pronouns, and descriptions) in 14:26 below.

". . . the Helper, the Holy Spirit, whom the Father will send in my name, he will teach you all things and bring to your remembrance all that I have said to you."

3. Write the names of the persons of the Trinity in the image:

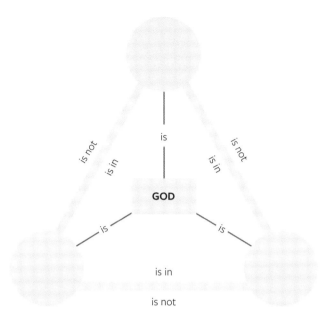

4. Which person of the Trinity is responsible for the roles listed below?

Physically speaks to the disciples (14:25)

Sends the Holy Spirit (14:26)

Asks for the Holy Spirit to be sent (14:26)

Gives His peace to the disciples (14:27)

Teaches the disciples all things (14:26)

Reminds the disciples of the teachings of Jesus (14:26)

Would be going away (14:28)

Obeys the commands of the Father (14:31)

The Trinity has a shared will, and each person of the Trinity has unique roles in carrying out that will as it pertains to our salvation and restoration. One of the purposes Jesus fulfilled on earth was to be the *physical* evidence of what the Father was like (Colossians 1:15). And the Holy Spirit, who would come to dwell in believers after Jesus ascended to heaven, would serve as the *spiritual* evidence—continually abiding in all Jesus's followers. All three persons of God are identical in character and equal in essence and *God-ness*.

Jesus knew the disciples would need the Holy Spirit to teach them and to remind them of what He had said. And in light of what was ahead for them, He knew they also would need His nearness and comfort.

5. What do you think Jesus meant when He contrasted His peace with the world's peace in 14:27?

6. Review 14:28–31.

When Jesus said the Father is greater, He reinforced their difference in roles. Jesus lived in willing submission to the Father—not because they weren't equal in *God-ness*, but because they had different roles in their plan for our salvation. He wanted the disciples to find comfort in—and rejoice in—the unity and diversity of the Trinity and the reality it made possible for them. This information was intended to fortify their faith!

The last two verses of John 14 almost seem to be passing information, but they're rich in theology.

7. **Fill in the table using 14:30–31. Use a Bible study tool if you need help.**

Who is the "ruler of this world"?	
Who does Jesus obey?	
What is the result of Jesus's obedience?	

"Rise, let us go from here" seems like a strange segue in the middle of a long conversation. Why would Jesus say that? It could've been that the rest of His teaching took place as they were preparing to leave but still in the house (similar to a midwestern goodbye). Or it's possible Jesus continued to teach as they walked to the garden of Gethsemane. Scripture isn't clear which it is, so use your sanctified imagination* over the next few days as we continue to study the Upper Room Discourse.

*A.W. Tozer called the sanctified imagination "the sacred gift of seeing, the ability to peer beyond the veil and gaze with astonished wonder upon the beauties and mysteries of things holy and eternal." See *The Best of A.W. Tozer, Book One*, comp. Warren Wiersbe (Camp Hill, PA: Wing Spread Publishers, 2000), 51.

John 15:1–17

 READ JOHN 15:1–17

1. *Review 15:1–5.*

Jesus often used the imagery around Him in His stories. So it's possible that as He made this seventh and final metaphorical *I am* statement—"I am the true vine"—they were near fruitful vines. Vines were a prominent sight in first-century Israel, and the disciples would've easily grasped the spiritual symbolism. In the Old Testament, the vine typically symbolized the nation of Israel, but Jesus called Himself the *true* vine. No longer were they to be rooted in the law or their nationality, but in Christ alone.

2. *Look up 15:2 in a Bible commentary to help you answer the questions below.*

What did Jesus mean by "takes away"?

What did He mean by "prune"?

Why would a person not bearing spiritual fruit need to be "taken away"?

Why would someone bearing fruit need to be "pruned"?

In our shortsightedness, pruning may seem unfair for those who are bearing fruit. But as painful as it may be to bleed, it's far worse to wither apart from the vine.

The disciples had already begun their cleaning or pruning process. Jesus referred to this when He washed their feet in 13:10 and connected His words to their cleansing. He had also promised them an ongoing relationship with God, and 15:4a clarifies that it's a mutual abiding—a two-way street. And this abiding implies an ongoing relationship; in Greek the word also means "remain, dwell, continue, tarry, to not depart."*

*See "G3306 - menō - Strong's Greek Lexicon (kjv)," Blue Letter Bible, accessed 5 July, 2024, https://www.blueletterbible.org/lexicon/g3306/kjv/tr/0-1.

3. Label the image below with the following: vine, branch, fruit.

_____

_____

_____

4. Draw lines to match the spiritual analogies.

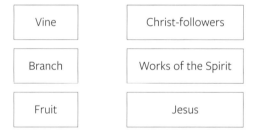

Vine	Christ-followers
Branch	Works of the Spirit
Fruit	Jesus

Look at the image above and imagine the branch being disconnected from the vine. That branch would no longer be able to sustain and grow fruit. The nutrients required to produce fruit don't come from the branch but from the vine. The good and necessary things that are coming to us come to us *through Him*!

When a branch constantly abides, it bears much fruit (15:5). This isn't only because of the fruit on the branch itself, but because of what that fruit contains: seeds. The fruit contains the vital components to make *more* fruit. The implication for effective multiplication and evangelism can't be overlooked in this illustration.

5. **Review 15:6–11.**

While 15:6 is sobering and convicting, don't let it evoke fear. Jesus wasn't unpacking an entire theological system; rather, He was making an important point: True disciples *abide* in Him.*

6. Let's look at how Jesus treated the branches in 15:2–8.

How are branches that aren't bearing fruit treated? (15:2)	
How are branches that aren't abiding in the vine treated? (15:6)	
What is the difference? Why do you think that is?	
In addition to bearing fruit, what would happen if the disciples abided? (15:7–8)	

In 15:9–11, Jesus repeated several themes He'd previously taught. Here, He showed them how the themes build on each other. True discipleship is linked to abiding, love, and obedience. The fullness of the joy of Christ is promised to those who understand and live out these themes.

7. How can abiding, love, and obedience lead to joy?

*David Guzik, "Study Guide for John 15 by David Guzik," Blue Letter Bible, last modified June 2022, https://www.blueletterbible.org/comm/guzik_david/study-guide/john/john-15.cfm.

8. Review 15:12–17.

Jesus's conversation shifts from the vertical connection between a disciple and the triune God to the horizontal connections between the disciples. The shift doesn't happen in a vacuum; the vertical and horizontal relationships are intrinsically intertwined as an overflow of the joy that comes from being a follower of Jesus. In fact, in this passage Jesus described His own love for the disciples to model how they ought to love one another

9. List all the ways Jesus loved the disciples in 15:13–16.

10. Based on what Jesus said in 15:12 and 15:17, what does He want us to do?

    A. Actively love other Christ-followers

    B. Actively love only people who worship like you

    C. Actively love only people who agree with your view of creation/end times

    D. Actively love only people who vote the way you vote

    E. Actively love only people who are in or above your socioeconomic bracket

John 15:18–27

 READ JOHN 15:18–27

1. Review 15:18–25.

Yesterday's study ended with Jesus talking about the importance of loving other believers; but today we see Him segue into hatred. The disciples were called to a radical life of love, obedience, and belief—and the people would hate them for it. Even though the topic was hatred, His tone seemed to be one of encouragement. He promised them that no disciple would navigate a path He hadn't first traveled. The world would hate them and the light they revealed, just as they hate Him, the very Light itself.

2. Fill in the blanks below from John 3:19–20.

"People loved the darkness rather than the light because _____ _____

____ _____."

"Everyone who does wicked things _____ ____ _____ and does not

come to the light, lest ____ _____ _____ ___ _____."

The world's hatred, though heavy and challenging, could also serve as encouragement because it meant they were walking in alignment with the Father's will, not in darkness!

3. When Jesus referred to the "world" in 15:19, who was He talking about?

- those who didn't know and love Him

- the planet itself

- those with obvious sin (drunkards, gluttons, sexually immoral)

Jesus came in flesh and did what only God could do, proving His deity in front of many onlookers—from the obvious sinners to the religious elite. But even witnessing His deity on display, many still didn't believe; therefore, there was no excuse for their unbelief. And not only did they fail to believe in Jesus, but they *hated* Him. And in a twist of irony, those who claimed to be experts in the Scriptures accidentally fulfilled a prophecy about Jesus through their hatred of Him (15:25).

4. Review 15:26–27.

All of Jesus's words about the world's hatred might have left His disciples discouraged if it weren't for His promise in these verses.

5. Draw lines and arrows on the diagram below indicating the following dynamics in 15:26–27 (it's okay for it to look messy):

- The Son sends the Holy Spirit to the disciples

- The Holy Spirit goes out from the Father

- The Holy Spirit bears witness about the Son (to the disciples)

- The Holy Spirit will bear witness about the Son (via the disciples)

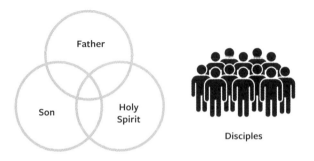

6. What have you learned or relearned about the Trinity this week that encourages you to be bold with the message of Christ?

Jesus had lived with His disciples from the start of His public ministry; they had witnessed it all. They heard His teachings, saw His miracles, were sent out in power, and knew better than anyone the character of the Man they called Rabbi. Their proximity to Jesus wasn't an accident; just like His death, it was the plan all along. The disciples would be among the first to proclaim the message of salvation to all nations. But these men wouldn't do it alone; they would walk in the fullness of Christ's joy provided by the presence of His Spirit. And even in persecution and hatred, they could rejoice—because He's where the joy is!

7. What stood out to you most in this week's study? Why?

8. What did you learn or relearn about God and His character this week?

Corresponding
Psalm & Prayer

 READ PSALM 91

1. What correlation do you see between Psalm 91 and this week's study of Jesus as God?

2. What portions of this psalm stand out to you most?

3. Close by praying this prayer aloud:

Father,
*   You answer me when I call. You rescue me when I'm in trouble.*
You draw near and give me Your salvation. You are my shield, my

fortress, and my refuge. You've already won the final battle, and I rejoice in Your victory.

Your Son said to not be troubled. And yet, even as I read His instruction, I don't always follow it. It's easy for me to get spun around in the tornado of my own fears instead of being held steady by a righteous fear of You. I've lost sight of my love for You, focusing on following rules while ignoring the state of my own heart.

Give me Your peace—not the world's cheap and fleeting kind, but Your true and eternal peace. Help me love better, not with fake love, but with Your love that sacrifices and abides. Teach me how to pray and remain faithful. Help me to recognize the Holy Spirit's guidance.

May I abide in Your shelter forever. Whatever comes my way— pruning or persecution—I know You will not fail. I surrender my life to You, Lord—every moment of my day, each decision I make, I yield my will and way to Your perfect will and way.

I love You too. Amen.

Rest, Catch Up, or Dig Deeper

 WEEKLY CHALLENGE

Sometimes the idea of loving God can feel abstract. This week, read through an overview of the *Sacred Pathways: Nine Ways to Connect with God* by Gary Thomas, and choose one of the ways you connect with God most easily. This isn't a stretching exercise, so don't choose one that's hard for you; choose the one you identify with most naturally! Write out a few ideas of how you can practice that "pathway" this week, then pick one and do it!

Scripture to Memorize

By this my Father is glorified, that you bear much
fruit and so prove to be my
disciples. As the Father has
loved me, so have I loved
you. Abide in my love.

John 15:8–9

John 16–17

The Encouragement of God

DAILY BIBLE READING

Day 1: John 16:1–15

Day 2: John 16:16–24

Day 3: John 16:25–33

Day 4: John 17:1–19

Day 5: John 17:20–26

Day 6: Psalm 98

Day 7: Catch-Up Day

Corresponds to Day 315 of *The Bible Recap.*

WEEKLY CHALLENGE

See page 203 for more information.

John 16:1–15

 READ JOHN 16:1–15

In this chapter, we continue studying Jesus's long monologue known as the Upper Room Discourse. He knew the hardships that awaited His disciples, and He also knew the wonderful, powerful things they would accomplish to glorify the Father, through Him, by the Spirit. He wanted to prepare them for both.

1. Review 16:1–4a.

2. Use a Greek lexicon to look up Strong's definition of the phrase *falling away* (16:1). Select the correct definition for this particular passage.

   A. To cause to distrust or desert someone he/she should trust or obey

   B. To entice another to sin

   C. To be annoyed

As the disciples listened, Jesus warned, "*You may lose favor in areas where you once had favor, you will be kicked out of the local worship gathering, and your very lives will be threatened or taken by those who believe they're being God's ambassadors. When all this happens, remember this conversation and don't fall away from what is true.*"

3. To see how Jesus's words proved true, read Acts 12:1–5 and write the outcome for the two disciples mentioned.

James:

Peter:

4. Review 16:4b–15.

Though the disciples were sad to hear that their Leader was leaving, Jesus comforted them by reminding them of the good news: In His absence, they wouldn't be left alone.

5. Fill in the blanks from 16:7 below.

"It is to your _____ that I ____ _____, for if I do not ____ _____,

the _____ will not come to you."

The Helper, the Holy Spirit, wasn't sitting in the heavenly dugout waiting for His turn to get in the game. The Holy Spirit—the third person of the Trinity—has always existed in unity with the Father and the Son, and He's been active in creation since the very beginning. Up until this point, the Spirit was sent to dwell *with* people for a specific purpose, but Jesus knew the bigger picture: The Spirit would come upon them in power, to dwell *in* them, equipping them for *every* good work. Let's zoom in briefly on what the Spirit has been up to so far.

6. Match the verse with the work of the Spirit.

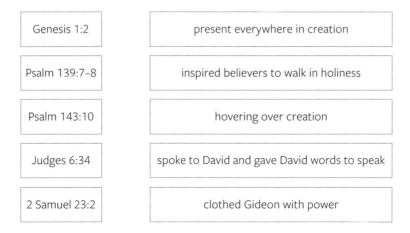

Genesis 1:2	present everywhere in creation
Psalm 139:7–8	inspired believers to walk in holiness
Psalm 143:10	hovering over creation
Judges 6:34	spoke to David and gave David words to speak
2 Samuel 23:2	clothed Gideon with power

Scripture helps us easily see that the Spirit has always had a specific purpose in the world, but His role would expand after Christ returned to heaven and the Father sent the Spirit to fill His people (Acts 2). And according to 16:8–10, it seems He would work in different ways, depending on His relationship with various people.

7. What three things is the Spirit focused on pointing out, according to 16:8?

8. In 16:9–10 below, circle the people mentioned who are connected to each focus.

- concerning sin, because they do not believe in me;

- concerning righteousness, because I go to the Father, and you will see me no longer;

- concerning judgment, because the ruler of this world is judged.

He would convict the perishing world ("they") concerning sin, helping them to believe in Jesus. He would convict believers ("you") of their righteousness, and He would convict "the ruler of this world" via judgment. All areas of His conviction serve to amplify His message to a dark world, inviting them to repent and escape the condemnation that comes with sin and judgment.

The Holy Spirit's conviction for believers isn't just about our sin—it's about our righteousness! He's reminding us of who we truly are in Christ (2 Corinthians 5:21). The Spirit will guide the disciples—and future believers—into all truth as He speaks in agreement with the Father and the Son, affirming their righteousness, which was granted to them by the finished work of Jesus.

9. If you're a follower of Christ, His Spirit dwells in you (Romans 8:9) and works to convict you of your righteousness (John 16:10). Describe a time when the Spirit has reminded you of your identity, steering you away from sin and toward your true identity as a child of God who walks in righteousness instead.

In His work, the Spirit always points to the other members of the Trinity (John 15:26). Much like Jesus, He doesn't show up with miracles simply to make a name for Himself—the members of the Trinity are always pointing to *each other*. The Spirit takes all that Jesus is and all the Father has and reveals it to those who belong to Him. With the fresh eyes granted to us by the Spirit, we can see this new reality and walk in truth—to the glory of God!

John 16:16–24

 READ JOHN 16:16–24

1. Review 16:16–19.

Have you ever found yourself listening to a lecture or a sermon that was way over your head? The disciples might have felt the same way as Jesus continued His discourse. In today's segment of the Upper Room Discourse, Jesus told them, *"I'll be gone for a bit and you won't see Me, and then I'll be gone again and then you'll see Me."* Imagine the disciples scratching their heads in confusion as they tried to decipher what He meant.

2. Use a Bible study tool to explain Jesus's words in 16:16. What two "little whiles" was Jesus referencing?

Jesus knew Calvary was right around the corner, and He knew His disciples needed more clarity that would come only from living through the experience. He also knew their hearts and minds required more than just direct information to endure all that would happen in the days ahead. As they sorted out their confusion among themselves, Jesus interjected with more teaching.

3. **Review 16:20–22** below. Underline any words related to sadness. Circle any words related to gladness.

> Truly, truly, I say to you, you will weep and lament, but the world will rejoice. You will be sorrowful, but your sorrow will turn into joy. When a woman is giving birth, she has sorrow because her hour has come, but when she has delivered the baby, she no longer remembers the anguish, for joy that a human being has been born into the world. So also you have sorrow now, but I will see you again, and your hearts will rejoice, and no one will take your joy from you.

Jesus understood sorrow. He knew what it was like to encounter the death of a friend (John 11:35), and He knew His disciples would be grieved at all that would take place. He also knew the great joy that was before them in the midst of hardship. And this promise wasn't just true for the disciples—it's a promise echoed throughout Scripture for all followers of Christ. The apostle Paul, who endured shipwrecks, beatings, a snakebite, and imprisonment, said, "In all our affliction, I am overflowing with joy" (2 Corinthians 7:4). It seems even the depth of our struggles can serve to magnify the goodness and nearness of God!

4. Have you experienced a time when God's goodness and nearness were more evident to you because of a struggle you were enduring? If so, briefly describe.

5. **Review 16:23–24.**

Here, Jesus talked to the disciples about their questions and desires, covering the past, present, and future.

6. Fill in the table below according to 16:23–24.

Phrase used	Complete the sentence	Circle the time period indicated
"In that day . . ."		past, present, future
"Whatever you ask the Father in my name . . ."		past, present, future
"Until now you have asked . . ."		past, present, future
"Ask and . . ."		past, present, future

Up to this point, the disciples had asked lots of questions and made their requests—mostly for things that might benefit them personally, like seats of honor in the kingdom of heaven (Mark 10:37). But Jesus called them to something greater, challenging them to ask in accordance with His will.

In giving them these instructions about asking in His name, He wasn't sharing the inside scoop on how they could get all they wanted in life. He wasn't instructing them to use the words "in Jesus's name" as the Christian version of *abracadabra* to command things to happen at their will. Instead, He was articulating two important aspects of prayer.

First, He was reiterating what He said previously in the Upper Room Discourse: They had a way to communicate with the Father, and *He* was the way (John 14:6). To approach the Father *in Jesus's name* is to be invited into conversation with the Father because of the relationship Jesus has made possible. It would be as if you were meeting your favorite author because your aunt happened to know him and arranged the meeting. You might name-drop and say, "I'm here because of my Aunt Darlene. She arranged this meeting with you." Likewise, believers can approach the Father in the name of His Son Jesus (Hebrews 4:14–16)!

Second, the essence of praying in His name is praying in accordance with His character and His will. In the ancient world, a person's name represented the whole of the person—their role, personality, and will. Praying in Jesus's name means praying for things that are aligned with who Jesus is and what Jesus wants (and Jesus wants what the Father wants).

Praying in Jesus's name is praying *like* Jesus, who said to the Father, "Your will be done" (Matthew 6:10).

7. Do you tend toward one of these extremes when you pray? If so, put a check mark beside it.

___ Command that God make things happen, because it's what you want.

___ Fret over asking Him for anything out of fear it *might* be outside of His will.

8. If it's the first, how can you reshape your posture of prayer to be in line with His example? If it's the second, write down one request you've been afraid to share with Him, then write out a prayer for that request.

Whether our prayers are answered with a yes or a no (or even a "wait"), we can trust that God always answers His kids and that His heart can be trusted. He wants us to ask Him for things (Matthew 7:7–11). God loves to say yes to His kids! And His no is also for our good. His plans will not be thwarted by our asking. When we pray in alignment with His will and we see Him actively at work through prayer, our joy will increase all the more!

John 16:25–33

 READ JOHN 16:25–33

1. Review 16:25–28.

Jesus didn't lighten the weight of His words as His lengthy talk with the disciples continued. Instead, He told them that when the time came—after the resurrection—He'd speak to them more plainly. *What a relief!*

2. Recall what we learned about prayer yesterday and summarize 16:26–27 in your own words.

They'd already been informed that they would be able to ask the Father "in His name," and here He was saying that His resurrection was what would make a way for them to talk to the Father. The Father loved them, He said. Jesus didn't have to convince an angry Father to be gracious and loving toward them; His death on the cross didn't turn the Father into a loving God. The Father has always been loving, has always been redeeming His kids! If you've been tempted to believe the lie that the Father is hostile and Jesus is loving, remember John 3:16: God so *loved* the world that He sent His only Son. And let the truth of 1 John 4:19—"we love him because he *first* loved us" (KJV, emphasis added)—correct any misguided thoughts.

190

Jesus was returning to this loving Father, who had both loved the Son *and* established His role as our Savior from before the foundation of the world (John 17:24, Revelation 13:8).

3. **Review 16:29–33.**

As Jesus taught, the disciples were starting to understand! They even plainly expressed their belief that Jesus came from God. But Jesus knew they would waver.

4. What warning did Jesus give the disciples in 16:32a? Complete the significance of this statement in the table below.

Warning (John 16:32a)	OT Prophecy (Zechariah 13:7)	NT Fulfillment (Matthew 26:56)

In 16:32b, Jesus reiterated the unity He shares with the Father. He comforted them (and possibly Himself) with the reminder that He would never be alone. The Father would always be inextricably united with Him—even through those lonely hours of His betrayal and death.

Through all these words—this unity with the Father, this promise of the Father's love—He was pointing them toward peace.

5. In capital letters (for emphasis), write the last five words of 16:33 in the ESV.

_____ _____ _____ _____ _____.

How could Jesus say, "I *have* overcome the world" when He hadn't yet finished what He was sent to do? When He spoke these words, He hadn't been to the cross yet; He hadn't conquered the grave. How could Jesus speak these words as though this had already happened?

Here's an interesting thought: Just as God isn't bound by location, He isn't bound by time either. After all, God invented time! And His omnipresence (being everywhere) means He can be both inside and outside of time (His creation) simultaneously, just as He can be both inside and outside the natural realm (which is also His creation).

6. **Read Revelation 13:8.** When was the Lamb of God slain?

This verse in Revelation helps articulate this point. Eternity-future had been accomplished in eternity-past. Jesus could say, *"I've already done this,"* because, as God the Son—one-third of our eternal Triune God—He wasn't only in the room with His disciples giving the Upper Room Discourse, but He was also in the future where His words had already been accomplished. *Wow!* (You might be feeling some connection to the disciples' confusion at this point—and that's okay! If you're unable to fully grasp some of these concepts, that's a great starting point for awe and wonder.)

And in the midst of this big, complicated, fresh news, Jesus still took the time to meet them right where they were, using a phrase He'd spoken during uncertain times before (Matthew 14:27), "Take heart." He could look in the faces of His disheartened disciples and tell them, *"It's all going to be okay; I've taken care of everything."* And that promise is true for you too.

John 17:1–19

 READ JOHN 17:1–19

John is the only gospel writer who recorded Jesus's High Priestly Prayer. As Jesus continued the Upper Room Discourse with His closest followers, He lifted His eyes toward heaven—a customary way of praying in those days—and addressed His Father personally. Notice the heart of Jesus in this prayer. He prayed for Himself—that He would glorify the Father—and then interceded for His disciples, as well as all those who would follow after them, including you! He kept His heart and mind fixed on the main thing, the Father's will, so that eternal life would come to others through Him.

1. Review 17:1–5.

2. Read Isaiah 42:8 and Isaiah 48:11. According to these verses, with whom will God share His glory?

3. Compare these verses to John 17:1–5. What does this tell you about the unity of God the Father and God the Son?

The opening petition of Jesus, "glorify your Son," implies that Jesus is God. God wouldn't share His glory with another, but He will share it within Himself through His Son. Jesus's entire ministry—His words and His works—brought glory to the Father; but the cross, which was a stumbling block for Jews and folly to the Gentiles (see 1 Corinthians 1:23–25), brought ultimate glory, because the cross was God's redemption plan all along.

Again, it's worth noting that Jesus—who is outside of time—was considering this work already accomplished (17:4).

4. Use a Greek lexicon to define *know* (17:3). Is this type of knowing transactional or intimate?

5. Review 17:6–10.

As Jesus continued His prayer, the disciples who overheard it had the unique benefit of not only learning more about the relationship within the Godhead (also known as the Trinity), but also witnessing the intensity and the intimacy of it. Can you imagine *hearing Jesus talk to the Father* about their relationship? The theme of this section reveals the unity they shared: Everything Jesus had was *from* the Father, and Jesus pointed everything back *to* the Father. And God's people—including us—are caught up in that story of love.

6. Read the paraphrase of 17:8 below slowly. Fill in the blanks using *Father, Son* (Jesus), and *the people*.

The _____ gave words to the _____. The _____ received the words and have come to know the words came from the _____ and the _____ believed that the _____ sent the _____.

7. How does this interaction between Father, Son, and people impact your view of your own salvation?

The Father made it known who would come to Jesus, and the Father also gave the Son words to speak. As these things happened, the Son continued crediting the Father. Jesus declared that all who are the Father's are also His, meaning that those who believe in Jesus belong to both of them. Just as Jesus points to the Father in all things, our lives should always point to Jesus. No one other than Jesus should be glorified by the things we do or say.

8. **Review 17:11–19.**

In verse 11, John recorded the only instance in Scripture where Jesus referred to the Father as "Holy Father." In other instances, Jesus used a more lighthearted *Abba* (Father) in prayer. This title, Holy Father, is a reminder for us that while we're invited to imitate Christ and confidently approach God the Father as *our* personal Father, we must do so with a right posture, remembering He is holy and worthy of reverence. Keep this in mind as you pray.

Jesus asked the Father to keep them (all believers) in His name. He didn't say, *"Keep them—but only if they earn it through the spiritual disciplines,"* or *"Keep them—but only if they're striving,"* or *"Keep them through an army of angels."* No. He prayed that God the Father would keep them through His mighty name. Your position as son or daughter is secure because it's protected by *the name greater than any other name.* You are held and kept by the eternal God. Keep this in mind as you remember your identity!

Jesus then prayed the Father would keep them in the world even as they were hated, and He asked that they'd be protected from the evil one. You, believer, are not of this world, but you are sent into this world, protected by the one who formed and sustains it. He will work in you and through you, and He will guard you as you go. Jesus also prayed that the Father would sanctify you through the truth of His Word (which is hopefully happening as you do this study!).

9. **Use a Bible dictionary to define *sanctify*. Then explain 17:19 in your own words. How does this take place in your own life?**

DAY 5

John 17:20–26

READ JOHN 17:20-26

Two thousand years ago, Jesus prayed for you before you even existed. God is never absent from us. And His thoughts are still on us. What exactly was He praying for you (and all those who'd believe in Him)? He yearned for a oneness between all believers, just as the three persons of God have oneness. His earnest prayer makes this evident as He emphasized unity and its effects.

1. Review 17:20–23.

2. Use the text to fill in the blanks on the circles below.

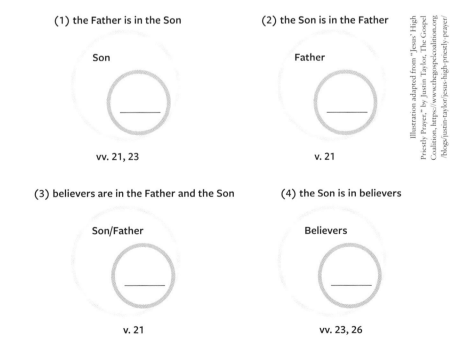

Illustration adapted from "Jesus' High Priestly Prayer," by Justin Taylor, The Gospel Coalition, https://www.thegospelcoalition.org /blogs/justin-taylor/jesus-high-priestly-prayer/

(1) the Father is in the Son

Son

———

vv. 21, 23

(2) the Son is in the Father

Father

———

v. 21

(3) believers are in the Father and the Son

Son/Father

———

v. 21

(4) the Son is in believers

Believers

———

vv. 23, 26

The relationship between the Father, Son, and Spirit has been compared to a dance. Can you picture it—the beautiful rhythm and delight among the three throughout the ages as they exist in perfect harmony, pointing in glory to each other? The Greek word *perichoresis*, literally meaning "circle dance," can be used to describe the Trinity's interactions with one another.* Jesus prayed that future believers would participate in this "dance" so that the world would see the beauty and believe in Him too (17:23).

3. **Read 1 Corinthians 12:12–14 and Ephesians 4:1–6.** What do these passages say about the relationship between believers? What are the roles of the Father, Son, Spirit, and believer in establishing peace?

In his book *The Reason for God* Tim Keller explains that self-centeredness is to cease dancing; it demands others orbit around us.† The life of the true believer is to be humble, self-sacrificing, and loving. As one delights in self-sacrifice and serving others, they begin to dance around the other, and when it's reciprocated, the other starts dancing too. This results in more beauty, deeper joy, greater delight!

*"What Is the Meaning of 'Perichoresis'?", Compelling Truth, https://www.compellingtruth.org/perichoresis.html.
†Timothy Keller, *The Reason for God: Belief in an Age of Skepticism* (New York: Penguin Books, 2018), 229.

4. Do you have a difficult time believing that God loves you with the same love with which He loves His Son (17:23)? If so, how do Jesus's words reshape your belief?

5. Review 17:24–26. Compare 17:24 to the words Jesus spoke earlier in John 14:2–3. What theme do you notice?

This unbreakable unity—within the Godhead itself *and* between God and His people—was the theme of Jesus's High Priestly Prayer and the very pinnacle of His Upper Room Discourse.

God is never absent from us. When He formed man and woman in the garden (Genesis 1:27), He didn't brush the dust off His hands and dismiss them. He walked with them in the garden (Genesis 3:8) and He sought them out (Genesis 3:9) when their sin and mistrust of His heart prompted them to hide. He is the God who is consistently *with* His people. One of the Son's names is Emmanuel, God with us (Matthew 1:23)! And at this point in His prayer, as the one who came to dwell prepared to return from where He'd come, He made it known: He wanted His people to dwell with Him too! Jesus expressed His desire that we would see the glory given to Him by the Father. It's another generous invitation from God to His kids.

Believer, we will spend eternity delighting in the glory of the magnificent God who formed us, loved us, saved us, and kept us. We will sing and dance with joy forever, because He's where the joy is!

6. What stood out to you most in this week's study? Why?

7. What did you learn or relearn about God and His character this week?

Corresponding Psalm & Prayer

 READ PSALM 98

1. What correlation do you see between Psalm 98 and this week's study of Jesus as God?

2. What portions of this psalm stand out to you most?

3. Close by praying this prayer aloud:

> *Holy Father,*
> *I praise You today—just like the roaring seas, the clapping rivers, and the singing hills. Your song of joy echoes through creation. You've sent Your salvation to the ends of the earth, and so I rejoice.*

You are righteous and faithful. You are steadfast love, and You have done marvelous things.

And even though in one moment I jump at the chance to praise You, in the next moment, I'm consumed by fear and silenced by timidity. I stumble, even when there's no block in my path. I confess that my heart has been fickle. I ask that You make me faithful.

Holy Spirit, remind me that I'm never alone. When I forget my identity as a child of God and wander off into sin, convict me of my true identity. Remind me of the righteousness that was granted to me because of the finished work of Jesus, and prompt me to walk in that righteousness. Sanctify me! And no matter what hardship comes my way on the righteous path, make me bold in declaring Your goodness.

When You answer my prayers with "yes," You are good. When You answer my prayers with "no," You are good. When You answer my prayers with "wait," You are good. So I surrender my life to You, Lord—every moment of my day, each decision I make, I yield my will and way to Your perfect will and way.

I love You too. Amen.

Rest, Catch Up, or Dig Deeper

 WEEKLY CHALLENGE

On Day 2, we see that none of the disciples lived under a cloud of sorrow because of Jesus's death and resurrection. Despite their difficult circumstances—and violent persecution—they remained joyful as they boldly proclaimed the good news and watched the Spirit at work. Read 1 Peter 1:3–9, then write a paragraph in your journal addressing this question: How does the living hope of Jesus's resurrection cause you to be filled with joy even in difficult circumstances?

John 18–19
The Passion of God

Scripture to Memorize

If you keep my commandments, you will abide in my love, just as I have kept my Father's commandments and abide in his love.

John 15:10

DAILY BIBLE READING

Day 1: John 18:1–27

Day 2: John 18:28–40

Day 3: John 19:1–16a

Day 4: John 19:16b–30

Day 5: John 19:31–42

Day 6: Psalm 88

Day 7: Catch-Up Day

Corresponds to Day 317 of *The Bible Recap.*

WEEKLY CHALLENGE

See page 228 for more information.

John 18:1–27

 READ JOHN 18:1–27

The final hours of Jesus's life are often called the passion narrative, because our English word *passion* comes from the Latin word for suffering. Everything we'll study this week is heavy, but take heart, because nothing we'll study this week happened outside of God's plan.

1. Review 18:1–11.

After He'd finished teaching His disciples, Jesus went to a garden. From other gospel accounts, we know that this is the garden of Gethsemane, located on Mount Olives—it's just outside the city gates, less than a thousand feet from the temple.

2. What three things did the soldiers and officers bring with them to the garden? What does this tell you about what they expected when they arrived?

As they walked with their lanterns and torches across the Kidron Valley, Jesus certainly would've seen them approaching, but He didn't run and hide. He knew His time had come, so He turned Himself over to them.

Making the final absolute *I am* statement in the book of John—this one was no metaphor—Jesus once again identified Himself as God by using the same language the Father used to identify Himself in Exodus 3:13–15.

3. In 18:6, what did the people who hear Jesus's proclamation of divinity do in response?

This is a common response to the revelation of divinity, but we see no indication that these men were worshiping Jesus. Did they fall down on purpose? Or was it a divinely orchestrated act, similar to the accidental prophecies made by some of Jesus's enemies? Scripture doesn't give us enough information to draw a clear conclusion, but we do know one thing: Falling down at the feet of Jesus is the proper response, whether intentional or accidental.

Simon Peter, who loved Jesus but didn't fully understand the plan yet, resisted the men who came to arrest Jesus. In what may have been an attempt to kill one of the men, Peter cut off the ear of a slave named Malchus. Luke's gospel tells us that Jesus told Peter to stand down and healed the man (Luke 22:51). Can you imagine being healed by the one you've come to arrest? And yet, they still arrested Jesus—and He willingly submitted.

4. Review 18:12–14.

The group did what they came to do and led Jesus away. They thought they'd captured Him, but He'd given Himself to them, as He was giving Himself for us. They didn't know they were leading Him to the moment when He would reconcile us to the Father.

Jesus went through a total of six trials—three religious and three civil—before His death; John recorded the first, fourth, and sixth.

In the first trial, Jesus met Annas. Rome replaced Annas as high priest with his son-in-law, Caiaphas, but a Jewish text called the Talmud tells us that Annas still had significant influence over Jerusalem's religious leaders.

He also was very likely in charge of the marketplace in the temple courts, where Jesus overturned the tables. So it's possible that this trial—which happened in the middle of the night and not in accordance with Jewish law—might have happened because Annas had a personal vendetta against Jesus.[*]

5. In 18:14, John reminds us of what Caiaphas said earlier in 11:50. Review 18:14 and complete it below.

It was Caiaphas who had advised the Jews that it would be expedient that

_____ _____ _____ _____ _____ _____ _____.

Caiaphas was playing a political game, not realizing he'd accidentally pointed to Jesus's reason for dying: substitutionary atonement.

6. Use a Bible dictionary or commentary to research the phrase *substitutionary atonement.* Then define it in your own words.

7. Review 18:15–18.

For the rest of our study today, we'll jump back and forth between what happened inside the high priest's quarters and what happened outside of it.

The servant girl who brought Peter into the high priest's courtyard asked him about his relationship to Jesus. The structure of the girl's question in Greek suggests she was curious, not accusatory. And still, Peter, who had just cut off an ear of the high priest's servant, cowered at her question. In his commentary on John's gospel, John Calvin wrote, "Our courage is of such a nature, that, of its own accord, it gives way where there is no enemy."[†]

---

[*]Tremper Longman III and David E. Garland, eds., *The Expositor's Bible Commentary: Luke–Acts Vol. 10,* rev. ed. (Grand Rapids, MI: Zondervan Academic, 2007), 614.

[†]John Calvin, *Commentary on the Gospel According to John,* trans. Rev. William Pringle, vol. 2 (Grand Rapids, MI: Christian Classics Ethereal Library), https://ccel.org/ccel/calvin/calcom35/calcom35.ix.viii.html.

Then Peter, fresh off his first denial of Jesus (see John 13:36–38), warmed himself around a charcoal fire alongside the officers and their servants.

8. Review 18:19–24.

Back inside, Annas questioned Jesus about His disciples (to understand how big His following was) and His teachings (to listen for something he could call blasphemous). Jesus's response likely would've reminded the religious leaders of Isaiah 45:19, and it meant that His message in private was always the same as His message in public.

9. Look back at 18:22. After Jesus invited them to bring witnesses to confirm what He said, what did one of the officers do? What did the man say?

10. What was the irony of the man's words?

    A. The man was himself a witness to Jesus's teachings

    B. The man didn't want to arrest Jesus in the first place

    C. Jesus is our ultimate High Priest, yet this man answered *Him* with a slap

11. Review 18:25–27.

As Peter warmed himself in the company of his Rabbi's arresting officers, more of them began to recognize him and question him. As lies often do, Peter's first lie turned into a second lie, which turned into a third. As Jesus stood through a farce of a trial on His way to pay the price for the sins of the world, one of His closest disciples denied ever knowing Him. And then, just as Jesus told him it would, the rooster crowed.

12. Read Luke 22:62. How did Peter respond when he realized what he'd done?

As it did for Peter, the gravity of our own sin should break our hearts.

13. As we close today, write a prayer of confession below.

John 18:28–40

 READ JOHN 18:28–40

When we left off in Jesus's trials yesterday, Annas had sent Jesus to Caiaphas, the current high priest. John didn't record an account of this trial, but from the other three gospels, we know that Caiaphas condemned Jesus. In ancient Israel, on the Day of Atonement each year, the high priest walked into the Holy of Holies—the most sacred place in the temple—to sprinkle the blood of a sacrificial lamb on the mercy seat of the ark of the covenant.

Caiaphas, whose job was to atone for the sins of the people of Israel, condemned the very one sent to atone for the sins of the world. But Caiaphas's condemnation only served to usher in God's plan from the beginning: the ultimate Day of Atonement. Jesus's perfect sacrifice as the *Great High Priest* meant that the Holy of Holies would no longer be needed.

After the trial with Caiaphas, there was another trial with the Sanhedrin, a panel of important religious leaders. Other gospel accounts tell us that not only did they find Jesus guilty, but they mocked Him. They spit on Him. They blindfolded Him and hit Him.

1. Review 18:28–32.

2. Did the religious leaders go into the governor's headquarters? What explanation for this did John give?

According to the regulations set out by the Pharisees, Jews who entered a Gentile building or home that had a roof on it were ceremonially unclean for a time and therefore had to be excluded from any holy observances. If the religious leaders entered Pilate's (the governor's) quarters, they wouldn't be able to eat the Passover feast.

3. Do a web search to find out what foods were traditionally included in first-century Passover meals, and either draw the items or list them on the plate below.

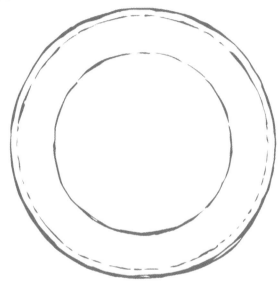

Eating the Passover lamb was so important to these leaders that they sent their prisoner—the Passover Lamb Himself—into Pilate's headquarters alone. As they separated themselves from God, the chasm between God and all of humanity was one step closer to being bridged.

During this first civil trial, Pilate tried to hand Jesus back to the Sanhedrin to be sentenced.

4. When Pilate attempted to get the religious leaders to sentence Jesus according to their own religious laws, how did they respond? Fill in the blanks from 18:31 below.

The Jews said to him, "It is _____ _____ for us to put anyone to

_____."

This was it. This was the reason Jesus was given to the Roman authorities. Rome had taken away the Jews' legal right to carry out capital punishment among their own people; in the Roman empire, only Roman authorities were allowed to execute prisoners.

And if Rome executed Jesus, it would be with the execution method they used almost exclusively for noncitizen criminals. There had been thousands of crucifixions by this point in the Roman empire's history, and because they wanted to deter future criminals, crucifixions were, by design, agonizing and shameful.

5. Review 18:33–40.

John didn't record Jesus's fifth trial with Herod but picked back up with His sixth—and final—trial. This was another trial with Pilate. The religious leaders wanted Rome to convict Jesus of political subversion, which was why Pilate asked Jesus, "Are you the King of the Jews?"

6. Using 18:33–37 as evidence, did Pilate think Jesus was a threat to Rome? Why or why not?

Facing a powerful official of the Roman empire, in quarters undoubtedly designed to dazzle and intimidate, Jesus—who lived a life of self-denial—described His eternal kingdom.

7. Read the following verses from Daniel. Match the Scripture reference to what it tells us about the kingdom of God.

Daniel 2:44	All peoples, nations, and languages should serve him
Daniel 7:14	His kingdom shall be an everlasting kingdom
Daniel 7:27	His kingdom shall never be destroyed, but will break other kingdoms into pieces

Fewer than five hundred years after Jesus told Pilate about His kingdom, the Roman empire fell. Empires, dynasties, and countries have risen and fallen since the beginning of time, and they'll continue to do so until the end. But Christ's kingdom is forever.

8. What question did Pilate flippantly ask Jesus in 18:38? Why is his question ironic?

During the Passover, Rome customarily released one prisoner back to the Jewish people. From John we know that Barabbas was a convicted thief, and from two other gospels (Mark 15:7; Luke 23:19) we know that he was also guilty of murder. Yet the people wanted him released, so he was set free, while Jesus took his place.

9. How are all believers like Barabbas?

John 19:1–16a

 READ JOHN 19:1–16A

1. *Review 19:1–11.*

With Jesus's final trial concluded, Pilate led Him away to be flogged—possibly to appease His accusers so they'd reconsider their call for His execution. When a person was flogged in the first century, it was with a whip that had broken bits of metal and bone tied to its leather straps. The naked prisoner's arms were tied around a stationary object like a pillar to confine him to one place and to pull his skin tight across his back. As the whip made contact with the victim's body, the sharp objects would embed themselves into the skin and were ripped free for the next lash. Strips of loose skin and tissue would hang from the places the whip tore.

Some church traditions teach that Jesus was whipped thirty-nine times, because Jewish law allowed up to forty lashes at a time. But these were Roman soldiers—they weren't bound by Jewish law. Historical accounts of flogging in the Roman empire say some were beaten so brutally their intestines were visible afterward. If this is what happened to Jesus, it would be consistent with the prophecy of Isaiah 52:14: "His appearance was so marred, beyond human semblance."

Jesus hadn't yet been sentenced to crucifixion, and yet the physical pain He endured had already exceeded anything most people will experience or can even imagine. But the pain was more than physical. God the Son—the King of the universe who came to serve and to save—was cruelly mocked.

2. Using 19:2–3 as your guide, fill in the table below. Use a study Bible if needed.

Object or Action	How the Soldiers Used It to Mock Jesus
Crown of thorns	
Purple robe	
Fake salute	

As he looked at Jesus—skin torn, bruised, and bloody, wearing only the garments shoved on Him in ridicule—Pilate likely wondered how this Man could possibly be a threat to Rome or to the Jews. So he presented Jesus to the chief priests.

3. What did Pilate say in 19:5 when Jesus came out?

Pilate said to them, "_____ _____ _____!"

4. How did the chief priests and officers respond in 19:6?

This was what the religious leaders wanted: a crucifixion. Even though Jews weren't legally allowed to enact capital punishment, there was a time when they could. Stoning was their execution method, and as cruel and barbaric as stoning seems to us today, it was a mercy in comparison with Rome's sadistic method of choice. *Crucifixion* comes from the same Latin root as our word *excruciating*, and it most certainly was. After the prisoner endured beatings, the nails that held him to the cross would rip through his wrists and feet. In agony, his joints would dislocate. Then he would suffer through a long death of suffocation, dehydration, and ultimately, heart failure. Calling for this death of torment, the religious leaders added the charge of blasphemy. John tells us that Pilate became "even more afraid" (19:8).

5. **Read Matthew 27:19 for additional context.** Why was Pilate already afraid to sentence Jesus to death?

When Pilate questioned Jesus further, Jesus told Pilate that he had authority to crucify Him only *because God gave it to him*. Jesus also said that the greater sin here wasn't Pilate's. Scripture doesn't tell us that all sins are equal; at some point in the history of Christianity, we began telling ourselves that. In 19:11, Jesus said the opposite: The sin of the one who turned Him over to His death was worse than Pilate's sin of sentencing Him to His death. Though all sins aren't equal in intent or impact, all sin does separate humanity from God. And this is why Jesus submitted Himself to physical, emotional, and relational torture: to make a way for us back to God, to restore what sin had broken.

6. **Review 19:12–16a.** In 19:12, how did the religious leaders pressure Pilate?

With this, the religious leaders had convinced him; Pilate cared so deeply about his political future that he was willing to sentence to death a Man he found no guilt in. So just at the time when the Passover lambs would be slaughtered, Pilate once again brought Jesus out and sat on a judgment seat.

7. What did Pilate say in 19:14 when he brought Jesus out?

He said to the Jews, "_____ _____ _____!"

This was the second time in this scene that Pilate told the religious leaders to *behold* Jesus. By saying, "Behold," Pilate meant, *"Don't just look at Him. See Him. Pay attention to Him."* And while he was likely only making a last-ditch effort to relieve himself of the burden of ordering Jesus's execution, his words meant more than he could have possibly known: *Behold! The King of the Universe, on His way to die a torturous death and bridge the gap between man and God, once and forever!*

John 19:16b–30

 READ JOHN 19:16B-30

Each gospel's writer shows Jesus through a particular lens. John's lens is "Jesus as God," but in today's passage, we see Jesus through all four lenses: King, Servant, Savior, and God.

There is much we can study about the historical context of the crucifixion—the archaeological evidence for where it took place, the linguistic nuances of the account, and the theological truths it teaches. But for the believer, when it comes to the cross of Christ, prayerful reading and contemplation is unmatched. Today, we'll slow down and take our time in the Word, reflecting on the great love of God and praying in response.

1. **Slowly reread 19:16b–22.**

Jesus is the eternal King. Pilate refused to change the inscription to sound like a claim; it was—and is—a fact. But it was only partially right. It should have read: *Jesus of Nazareth, the Eternal King of the Universe.*

2. Write a prayer of praise to the KING of the universe.

3. **Slowly reread 19:23–24.**

Jesus is the Savior. He fulfills all of Scripture—like when Psalm 22 pointed to the soldiers casting lots for His garments, and when Genesis 22 pointed to the sacrifice that the LORD would provide. Jesus is the final sacrificial lamb, and for our sins, He died.

4. Write a prayer of confession to the SAVIOR of the world.

5. **Slowly reread 19:25–27.**

Jesus came to serve. With some of Jesus's final agonizing breaths, He made sure that His mother—very likely a widow at this point, with little means—would be cared for. Even in His suffering, He provided and He blessed.

6. Write a prayer to the one who came as a SERVANT, asking for His provision and blessing.

7. **Slowly reread 19:28–30.**

Jesus is God. Nothing in Jesus's life or death happened outside of God's will. And since God the Father, God the Son, and God the Spirit are always in perfect unity, nothing in Jesus's life or death happened outside of *Jesus's* will. Before the foundation of the world, God had a plan to bring us back to Himself. When Jesus said, "It is finished" (19:30), His cruel and agonizing death was over. More than that, the work He came to do had been perfectly accomplished. God's plan is always the best plan, and His will is always right.

8. Write a prayer to the GOD of the universe, yielding your will to His perfect will.

John 19:31–42

 READ JOHN 19:31–42

1. Review 19:31–37.

When someone was crucified, he had to push himself up with his legs to be able to breathe. Breaking his legs would bring on a quicker death. Jesus was already dead when the soldiers broke the legs of the other two on their crosses. As John wrote, this fulfilled the words of Scripture: "He keeps all his bones; not one of them is broken" (Psalm 34:20). It was important that His bones weren't broken not only to fulfill these particular words in Scripture, but to fulfill a bigger picture as well.

2. Read Exodus 12:46 below and underline the part of the passage that points to John 19.

> [The Passover lamb] shall be eaten in one house; you shall not take any of the flesh outside the house, and you shall not break any of its bones.

3. Read 1 Corinthians 5:7 below and underline the part of the passage that shows how Jesus fulfilled this.

> Cleanse out the old leaven that you may be a new lump, as you really are unleavened. For Christ, our Passover lamb, has been sacrificed.

4. In 19:34, what two liquids came out of Jesus's body?

_____ and _____

The pericardium is the fluid-filled sac around the heart, and of course, all blood flows through the heart. When the soldier's spear pierced both the pericardium and the heart, the contents of each flowed out. Maybe, like Augustine argued, the blood and water represented the sacraments of communion and baptism. Or maybe, like Calvin wrote, they represented justification and sanctification.* Or perhaps this terrible moment was burned in John's memory, and he wanted us to understand that Jesus, who was fully man, had truly died.

5. Review 19:38–42.

After a crucifixion, Roman officials typically left the body on the cross for days as it decayed, allowing wild animals to feast and grotesquely deterring potential offenders from crime. Eventually, unclaimed bodies would be thrown into a common pit. But God's law prohibited bodies from being left on trees overnight (Deuteronomy 21:22–23). So Pilate allowed two unlikely men to move Jesus's body.

6. Who were the two men who helped provide for Jesus's burial? Write what you know about them below.

Joseph of Arimathea	Nicodemus (go back to Week 1, Day 4 for a refresher)

---

*John Calvin, *Commentary on the Gospel According to John*, trans. Rev. William Pringle, vol. 2 (Grand Rapids, MI: Christian Classics Ethereal Library), https://ccel.org/ccel/calvin/cal com35/calcom35.ix.viii.html.

For Joseph and Nicodemus, their fears hindered their faith while Jesus was alive. But in His death, their hearts were changed, and they moved from darkness into the light.

7. Cross out the things below that 19:41–42 *doesn't* teach us about the tomb.

- The tomb was new.

- The site of the tomb is now marked by the Church of the Holy Sepulchre.

- The tomb was in a garden.

- The site of the tomb is close to a hill that looks like a skull outside of the Damascus Gate of Jerusalem.

- The tomb was close to the place of crucifixion.

There are at least two prominent sites in Jerusalem that Christians believe may be the site of Jesus's death and burial. And while various convincing arguments have been made, we don't know for sure where His tomb was, because the Bible doesn't tell us, and because *He's not there.*

We began our reading this week with Jesus's arrest and ended with His body lying in a borrowed tomb. Everything we studied this week was heavy, but we must understand the bad news before we can fully understand the good news. For instance, "You have a surgery appointment with the best brain surgeon in the world in fifteen minutes," sounds terrifying or absurd unless you know you have a potentially fatal brain tumor.

The bad news is that our sin means we deserve death and eternal separation from God. The good news is that the one who never sinned is the one who took our place, defeated death, and restored us back to God.

In 1771, William Cowper wrote the bad news and the good news in a hymn called "There Is a Fountain Filled with Blood":

> There is a fountain filled with blood
> Drawn from Immanuel's veins;
> And sinners, plunged beneath that flood,
> Lose all their guilty stains.

8. In your own words—and maybe even as a poem—write the bad news and the good news.

Even when we read about His death, Jesus is our good news, and He's where the joy is!

9. What stood out to you most in this week's study? Why?

10. What did you learn or relearn about God and His character this week?

DAY 6

Corresponding
Psalm & Prayer

 READ PSALM 88

1. What correlation do you see between Psalm 88 and this week's study of Jesus as God?

2. What portions of this psalm stand out to you most?

3. Close by praying this prayer aloud:

Father,
    Sometimes the darkness seems too much to bear.
    Like the psalmist, Jesus was overwhelmed with sorrow. Yet—knowing all that would happen to Him—He gave Himself over to the plan for redemption.

Like the psalmist, Jesus's friends had forsaken Him. Yet—knowing all along what they would do—He loved them, taught them, and served them. He washed their feet.

Like the psalmist, Jesus was close to death. Yet on the cross, He continued in His suffering until death to make us right with You.

I am Peter. I am not threatened, but I have denied You.

I am Barabbas. I am the sinner, but You took my place on the cross. You bore the wrath for my sins.

Even when my soul is full of troubles, even when despair seems to have won, even when darkness closes in, remind me that the story isn't over. Remind me that Your Son is coming back.

As I wait for the glorious rest of the story, may I keep turning to You, every morning and every night. Come quickly, Lord. I surrender my life to You, Lord—every moment of my day, each decision I make, I yield my will and way to Your perfect will and way.

I love You too. Amen.

Rest, Catch Up, or Dig Deeper

 WEEKLY CHALLENGE

Choose a hymn about the crucifixion of Jesus. (Do a web search for some suggestions if you need them.) Every day for a week, let that hymn be the first song you play in the morning and the last song you play before sleeping. Each time you listen, pray as the Spirit leads you.

John 20–21
Eternal Life with God

DAILY BIBLE READING

Day 1: John 20:1–18

Day 2: John 20:19–31

Day 3: John 21:1–14

Day 4: John 21:15–19

Day 5: John 21:20–25

Day 6: Psalm 42

Day 7: Catch-Up Day

Corresponds to Day 319 of *The Bible Recap*.

WEEKLY CHALLENGE

See page 252 for more information.

John 20:1–18

 READ JOHN 20:1–18

1. Review 20:1–10.

2. It's time to break out your investigative skills. Write down at least three pieces of evidence from these verses that point to Jesus's resurrection.

1.	
2.	
3.	

This evidence is important because it revealed Jesus's body was not *stolen*—He was *risen*.

The absence of a body is certainly remarkable but not enough to substantiate a miracle. Rolling away the stone placed at the entrance of the tomb would've required multiple men. This is strong, but still not conclusive. It's important for us to examine those graveclothes.

People were buried wrapped in strips of linen cloth lined with embalming oils and spices. The cloth hardened as these embalming materials dried, creating a mummy-like, papier-mâché effect. Remember when Lazarus was raised from the dead? People had to assist him in getting out of the cloths—either cutting or tearing the linen strips. John's phrasing implies that none of this had occurred in Jesus's case. The linen cloths were left in order and undisturbed.

Additionally, the face cloth was folded and left behind as if someone were doing laundry. Thieves don't have a reputation for wasting time at the crime scene, tidying up to leave things better than they found them. Nor would thieves have left behind linen cloths coated in expensive embalming spices.

All evidence pointed to a miracle! However, the disciples didn't get it just yet. John "believed," but the full revelation of Jesus's identity still wasn't clear. But we're getting there.

3. Review 20:11–18.

After their race to the tomb (John makes sure to mention that he won) and subsequent investigation, John and Simon Peter headed home. But Mary Magdalene did no such thing. We can't rush past Mary's garden experience. This is no average sunrise walk.

4. Complete the sentences below to follow Mary's search for Jesus's body.

Mary _____ _____ outside of the tomb.

Mary _____ to look inside the tomb.

Mary _____ two angels.

Mary _____, "They have taken away ____ _____, and I do not know
 where they have _____ _____."

Notice the emotional distress Mary was in. Her obsession with finding Jesus's body was all-consuming. The presence of the disciples didn't calm her. The empty tomb didn't satisfy her. Even the presence of two angels didn't appease her. *Who sees two angels and doesn't even care?* A woman on a mission for *one thing*.

5. Read Exodus 25:18–19. Where were the cherubim seated at the mercy seat? Where were the angels seated in John 20:12?

The mercy seat of the temple was the very place of God's presence. But only one priest could approach once a year. At the empty tomb, two angels sat in the same position. Except this time, there was no veil and no stone limiting access. God's presence was no longer contained to one spot for one priest. Jesus is God, and His resurrection made it possible for all to enter. Mary was about to get the first glimpse.

6. Read Romans 10:17. How do you see this active in John 20:16?

Many have theorized why Mary didn't recognize Jesus at first. But perhaps in His divine wisdom, Jesus was reserving a more profound lesson for all of us. Jesus didn't reveal His identity by speaking *His* name but by speaking *hers*. Remember John 10:27? Mary recognized the voice of her Good Shepherd, and her search reached a better end than she could have imagined: Jesus was alive!

Mary's joy seemed to overflow a little too much, as Jesus asked her to stop clinging to Him. (Side note: This little detail confirmed that Jesus was no ghost or risen spirit, but a real body risen to real life. Mary couldn't cling to Casper.) They both had work to do, and it was time they got to it.

7. Look back at John 1:12–13. How was this fulfilled in 20:17?

Jesus had never referred to the disciples as "brothers" before. His resurrection secured a new relationship. As believers in Jesus, we're more than servants, more than disciples, more than friends; we're grafted in as Jesus's brothers and sisters—sons and daughters in God's diverse and divine family!

8. Faith in God's identity and our own comes through hearing God's Word. We must allow the Holy Spirit to expose the lies and speak the truth. Slow down and practice some listening prayer. Use this table to help get you started.

Lie	Truth
Example: I am unloved.	*Jeremiah 31:3—"I have loved you with an everlasting love."*

This garden conversation concluded with Mary being sent on a mission: "*Go tell the boys I am ascending.*" Jesus would never die again. He rose to a new life—an eternal one.

Mary left the tomb with the message that has traveled from that quiet garden through the streets of Jerusalem; it has persevered through persecution, traveled across cultures and continents, and been faithfully passed down through centuries of saints and sinners to reach you wherever you're reading this study today. "*I have seen the Lord! He is alive!*" Let all who believe rejoice!

John 20:19–31

 READ JOHN 20:19–31

1. *Review 20:19–23.*

The disciples were huddled in grief—doors locked, fear palpable. And Jesus entered miraculously into their midst with the first words they had heard Him utter since before the cross, "Peace be with you." Imagine their relief and consolation when their desertion of Jesus was met with a blessing. This is our God.

2. *Compare 20:19–22 to Acts 2:1–4.* What similarities do you find? What questions does this bring up?

3. *Using a Greek lexicon, define pneuma.* Where do you see *pneuma* in both passages?

The words "receive the Holy Spirit" could be confusing. Did they receive the Spirit here or in Acts? Was John contradicting Acts?

D. A. Carson gave great insight in his commentary *The Gospel According to John*: "Jesus' 'exhalation' and command *Receive the Holy Spirit* are best understood as a kind of acted parable pointing forward to the full enduement still to come."* In layman's terms, when Jesus exhaled on them and referred to the Holy Spirit, He was giving a physical representation (or "acted parable") of a spiritual reality yet to come.

He breathed the promise of the Holy Spirit on them so that *when* they heard the wind in the upper room at Pentecost, they would know it was the Breath of Life (*pneuma*). In Genesis 2:7, God first breathed life into man. Here, God was breathing a resurrected *new* life over His disciples—the presence of Christ now forever available in the person of the Holy Spirit.

4. In 20:23, Jesus revealed what the Spirit would empower them to do. Compare this promise to the end of Peter's message in Acts 2:38.

John 20:23	Acts 2:38
If you _____ the sins of any, they are _____ them; if you withhold _____ from any, it is withheld.	And Peter said to them, "_____ and be baptized every one of you in the name of Jesus Christ for the _____ of your sins, and you will receive the gift of the Holy Spirit."

Jesus was not implying that the Holy Spirit now gave the disciples power to offer (or withhold) forgiveness of sins for the salvation of souls. That is a job reserved for God alone. Rather, He was revealing that the outpouring of the Holy Spirit will compel and empower us to share the gospel of Jesus Christ (and the offer of His forgiveness) with the world. Someone has to speak up about salvation for people to know forgiveness is possible (Romans 10:14)! As the Father sent Jesus into the world with the message of repentance, so now the Spirit sends us.

*D. A. Carson, *The Gospel According to John* (Grand Rapids, MI: William B. Eerdmans Publishing Company, 1991), 655.

In Acts 2, the Spirit descended, and Peter started preaching. In 20:26, the disciples still had the doors locked. We aren't at the full spiritual outpouring just yet.

5. Review 20:24–29. What title has our culture assigned to Thomas because of this one interaction? What have we been calling him in this study instead?

Thomas may have doubted (and in fact, *all* the disciples doubted), but at least he was honest about it. He wasn't going to pretend he believed when he didn't. His honesty didn't repel Jesus—it drew Him closer. Perhaps Thomas's story wasn't recorded as a mockery but as a model for how to handle doubt. In the same way that Jesus handled Thomas's doubt with love, your questions are safe with Him.

6. Are there passages of Scripture that you're only pretending to believe? Follow Thomas's example and get honest with God; write it down and ask Him to reveal the truth.

Thomas's doubt was kindly corrected, and he responded with recognition, "My Lord and my God!" And then, the sweetest blessing flowed from Jesus's mouth right into the lives of future generations of saints (including us!): "Blessed are those who have not seen and yet have believed." This is the blessing now spoken over each and every believer. What a blessing! What an encouragement!

7. Review 20:30–31.

John ended chapter 20 with a reminder of why he was writing: *"All I want is for you to believe in Jesus. His teaching, signs, and resurrection all reveal one thing—He is God. Believe and truly live."*

DAY 3

John 21:1–14

 READ JOHN 21:1–14

1. Review 21:1–3.

It's important to slow down and attentively engage with this final revelation of Jesus so we don't miss the rich, redemptive work happening here. Today is all about the setup, so let's start with a quick "Where? Who? What?"

2. *Where* are they? On the map below, circle the Sea of Tiberias. Draw a line from Jerusalem to the sea.

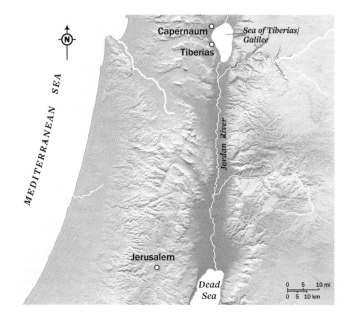

You may be thinking, *Sea of Tiberias? I thought it was called the Sea of Galilee!* And you'd be right. The Sea of Galilee went by (and still goes by) many names—Sea of Tiberias, Lake of Gennesaret, Lake Kinneret, Sea of Ginosar, Waters of Gennesareth, et cetera. Groups of people would call it by different names depending on who was the ruling authority at the time. The Sea of Tiberius was its Roman name. The Sea of Galilee was what the locals called it.

3. *Who* was by the sea? Using 21:2 as your guide, fill in the Galilee guest list with the correct RSVP below. Hint: You may need to use a Bible study tool to identify the right disciples by their nicknames.

Disciple	RSVP		
Simon Peter	Yes	No	Maybe
Philip	Yes	No	Maybe
John the apostle	Yes	No	Maybe
Andrew	Yes	No	Maybe
Nathanael	Yes	No	Maybe
Matthew	Yes	No	Maybe
James of Alphaeus	Yes	No	Maybe
Simon the Zealot	Yes	No	Maybe
Thomas	Yes	No	Maybe
Judas Iscariot	Yes	No	Maybe
Judas (not Iscariot)	Yes	No	Maybe
James	Yes	No	Maybe

4. *What* was going on? Why were the disciples in Galilee?

If you wrote "going fishing," you're partially right. But they probably didn't make the 100-mile trek from Jerusalem just to throw a few nets in the water. In Matthew 26:32 and 28:10, Jesus told the disciples that He would meet up with them in Galilee after His resurrection. In Mark 16:6–8, the angels relayed the same message. They took Jesus seriously, waiting in obedient expectation beside the sea.

5. Review 21:4–7a. Why do you think they didn't recognize Jesus initially?

6. Read Luke 5:3–11. Which soon-to-be disciples were present in this story?

7. Review John 21:7b–11.

Perhaps it was still too dark outside to recognize Jesus. Perhaps they were all a bit drowsy. Perhaps Peter was nearsighted. What we do know is that only one person had ever miraculously provided this big of a catch before by having them cast their nets on the other side. Imagine John's eyes widening in recognition as his muscles strained to haul in the net: "*Wait a second, we've done this before. Peter! It's the Lord!*"

Peter put on his tunic (as the boys were likely fishing sans clothing) and threw himself into the sea toward his Savior.

John includes an interesting detail about this massive haul of fish: There were 153 of them. Fishermen often sold their catch by weight, so the *number* of fish likely wouldn't have been worth noting—unless it represented something more important.

8. Look up Luke 5:10. What did Jesus say these fishermen would be catching?

This specific of fish in the disciples' abundant catch seems to point back to the promise Jesus made when He originally called these men to follow Him. And while Scripture doesn't give us evidence, it has been said there were 153 species of fish in the world at the time, and some believe these fish were one of each species—representing Jesus's call to make disciples of all nations (Matthew 28:19–20) and the promise that His kingdom includes those from every nation, tribe, people, and language (Revelation 7:9). Fishers of men indeed!

9. Review 21:12–14.

10. Every detail of Scripture is important, even if it seems to only describe brunch. Use 21:4–14 as a reference to answer the following questions.

- What kind of fire was waiting for them on the shoreline?

- What two items were on the menu?

- What time of day was it?

Have you ever tasted a dessert that immediately reminded you of your childhood? Have you ever walked past a stranger, caught a whiff of their cologne, and felt a hint of sadness because it reminded you of your grandfather? This is a legitimate scientific phenomenon. The same part of the brain that processes our senses is also partly responsible for storing emotional memories.

All of these tastes and aromas recorded in 21:4–14 would've snapped the disciples into real and raw memories. The smell of the sea was the signature scent of most of their time spent with Jesus. The last time Jesus broke bread with them was in the upper room. Perhaps they recalled His miraculous feeding of the five thousand as He prepared the fish.

And then there was the charcoal fire. This word *anthrakia* is only recorded twice in all of Scripture: here and in John 18:18. As far as we know, the last time Peter stood around a charcoal fire—in those cold, late-night hours before the crucifixion—he denied even knowing Jesus. This aroma could not have been pleasant for him. How difficult was it to reunite with Jesus around a place of such vulnerability and shame?

And that was just the point. Jesus was setting the table for a whole feast of redemption. We'll get to participate in that full-course meal tomorrow.

John 21:15–19

 READ JOHN 21:15–19

Peter was about to learn that Jesus was doing much more than making breakfast. He was graciously restoring their relationship and clarifying Peter's calling.

1. *Review 21:15–17.* Who or what do you think *these* in 21:15 referred to?

Perhaps Jesus was gesturing to the 153 fish they'd just caught. Maybe He was pointing to the other disciples. Maybe Peter really loved bread. We can't know for sure. What we do know is Jesus was being intentional about the entry point of Peter's calling. He was about to receive a great assignment, a heavy calling. Jesus was anchoring Peter in the underlying and sustaining motivation of fruitful ministry—a love for Jesus above and beyond anything else.

2. Using 21:15–17 and a Greek lexicon, complete the following table.

Jesus's Question	Greek Word for Love	Definition	Peter's Response	Greek Word for Love	Definition
"Simon, son of John, do you love me more than these?"			"Yes, Lord; you know that I love you."		
"Simon, son of John, do you love me?"			"Yes, Lord; you know that I love you."		
"Simon, son of John, do you love me?"			"Lord, you know everything; you know that I love you."		

In the English language, we have only one word for "love." We know all loves aren't created equal. For example, you (hopefully) love your family differently from how you love pizza. And yet, we still "love" both.

In Greek, there are four words to communicate four different kinds of love—*philia*, *eros*, *storge*, and *agape*.

Notice Jesus used *agape* in the first two questions while Peter responded with *philia*. It was as if Jesus was saying, *"Peter, do you love Me unconditionally and eternally?"* And Peter responded with, *"Yes. I think You're awesome, friend."* Maybe Peter was scared to voice a love he'd failed to show in the past. But did you see the shift that happened in their third exchange? Jesus picked up Peter's use of *philia* instead.

Why? Was Jesus decreasing His call? Was He settling for a lesser love?

No. Jesus was meeting Peter where he was. He knew what lay ahead for Peter, and He had to ensure that the love they shared was the foundation for the work Peter was being assigned. Not guilt. Not shame. Not obligation. *Love.* Instead of continuing to question Peter's *agape*, Jesus modeled what it looked like. How kind and compassionate of our God not to discipline us when we need loving assurance.

3. Do you doubt God's love for you because of something you did, something done to you, or something someone spoke over you? Take a moment to write down whatever it is as a prayer of confession.

4. Now reread the exchange between Peter and Jesus, recognizing that the same patience and attention Jesus offered Peter is available to you. Write out a prayer of gratitude for His love for you, and commit to receiving it.

5. Now that we've got the "loves" straight, let's focus on the commands. Using 21:15–17 and a Greek lexicon, complete the following table.

Fill in the Blanks	Define
Feed my _____.	Feed—
Tend my _____.	
_____ my _____.	Tend—

Notice the progression of Jesus's commands.

First, Peter was to focus on feeding the lambs—the ones new to a life of following Jesus, the weak, the vulnerable. They would need specific care. At some points they would need to be carried. And hadn't Jesus done that for Peter? Was He not doing it here?

Peter would also need to "tend" the sheep. This word communicated leadership, a "staying with" and "staying beside." Fishermen had no need to keep a relationship with fish. You caught them, counted them, then sold them. Shepherds were different. They walked with their sheep from birth—across rocky hills and arid mountains, sleeping amid the fold and protecting them every step of the way. Bottom line: *Shepherds stay.*

Lastly, he'd feed the sheep. Shepherds always strove to get the mature sheep to a place of plenty, an oasis area where they could learn to feed themselves, drinking deeply of natural springs in the desert. Peter was being sent on a mission to get people to this same level of spiritual maturity, eventually learning to come to the Source of living water for themselves.

6. Review 21:18–19. Do a quick web search to see how Peter eventually died.

Jesus ended Peter's restitution with a sobering image he would not get until much later. But with His final "Follow me," Jesus gave us all a simple model for discipleship. Even as we lead, even as we feed and teach others, even as we die, we are to follow Him every step of the journey. Jesus, our kind, patient, compassionate, and victorious God, has already made the way.

John 21:20–25

 READ JOHN 21:20-25

1. Review 21:20–22.

2. What was the last thing Jesus said to Peter in 21:19? What was the first thing Peter did in 21:20?

We could easily get frustrated with Peter. But the truth is, we're often like him—turning from the words of our Savior to make sure we've got an eye on what everyone else is doing. Jesus was quick with His loving correction, repeating the phrase that would come to define the rest of Peter's life, "You follow me."

3. Using a Greek lexicon, look up and define *follow me.*

Jesus used this phrase six times in John's gospel. In Greek, the root word is *alpha*, meaning "beginning." John started his book by getting us to look to the Word, who "was in the beginning." Being the brilliant storyteller that he was, that is also where he ended. We follow the Alpha and the Omega—the one who always was, always is, always will be (Revelation 22:13).

Like Peter, most of our missteps in following Jesus come down to a matter of focus—we start looking to the wrong people, we get distracted, we get off track. But the guidance remains just as direct and just as clear for every believer: "Follow me." Sometimes the directions are so simple we feel like there must be more. But this is it! Follow Jesus. End of story (literally).

4. To help us refocus, circle all the commands in Proverbs 4:25–27 below.

> Let your eyes look directly forward,
>   and your gaze be straight before you.
> Ponder the path of your feet;
>   then all your ways will be sure.
> Do not swerve to the right or to the left;
>   turn your foot away from evil.

5. What are some things that distract you from following Him? Be specific.

6. Review 21:23–25.

In 21:23, John cleared up a couple of rumors. Jesus was not insinuating that John would never die; He was simply telling Peter that John's future was none of his business. So if you got excited to look for John in your local congregation this coming Sunday, you'll be disappointed.

7. You may have seen a familiar word in 21:24. As a refresher, circle the correct definition below.

    A. An embellished story used to make people emotional

    B. A word from God to be shared in the middle of a service

    C. The story of how my life changed after I got saved

    D. A personal story that primarily points to Jesus and how He is revealed through my life

John launched out with a testimony back in 1:19—JTB's testimony of Jesus—and concluded with his own. Throughout this entire gospel, John's emphasis was clear: *Jesus is God. Look at Him.* He goes so far as to not even mention his own name the entire book. By calling himself "the disciple whom Jesus loved," John took the focus off himself to become lost behind the love of Jesus. This is our example.

The final words of John's gospel end like a brilliant screenplay. If this were a movie, the viewer would be left expecting sequels. *If there are more signs like this, let's have them!*

And so we would. Centuries of saints would follow who would keep telling the story—from the Acts of the Apostles, to the missionary journeys of Paul, sailing from the island of Patmos, flowing down the rivers of Africa, even finding their way into our news feeds today. What miraculous acts of preservation! What a story carried along by the Holy Spirit! But no matter the book, continent, or conveyance, one unmistakable message echoes from every page: This has only ever been about Jesus. He's where the joy is!

8. What stood out to you most in this week's study? Why?

9. What did you learn or relearn about God and His character this week?

Corresponding
Psalm & Prayer

 READ PSALM 42

1. What correlation do you see between Psalm 42 and this week's study of Jesus as God?

2. What portions of this psalm stand out to you most?

3. Close by praying this prayer aloud:

Father,

    You are my salvation and my God. I will praise You! During the day, You surround me with Your steadfast love. At night, Your song is with me.

If every good thing You've ever done was written down, the world couldn't hold all the books that would be filled.

But like Mary, I have despaired. Like Thomas, I have doubted. Like Peter, I have been distracted. And like David, I have been downcast. I've wondered if You cared for me. I've questioned Your promises. And I haven't always taken my uncertainties and fears to You, the only one who can dispel them. Forgive me.

Remind me of Your past faithfulness, and let that encourage my hope. Remind me that Jesus is my brother, and let that build my trust. Remind me that You defeated death, and let that grow my courage.

Teach me to follow You. I surrender my life to You, Lord—every moment of my day, each decision I make, I yield my will and way to Your perfect will and way.

I love You too. Amen.

Rest, Catch Up, or Dig Deeper

 WEEKLY CHALLENGE

On Day 4, we took a quick look at how Peter died. Peter is one of millions who have given up their lives for the sake of the gospel. This week, do some additional study and find at least three more martyrs in three different generations of church history. (If you want a deeper challenge, consider reading *Foxe's Book of Martyrs* by John Foxe.) While you will probably never be crucified for your beliefs, these stories inspire boldness and remind us of the exceeding value of Jesus. May you be encouraged to courageously follow Jesus all the days of your life!

FOR GROUP LEADERS

Thank you for using this study and leading others through it as well! Each week has a wide variety of content (daily Bible reading, content and questions, Scripture memorization, weekly challenge, and resources) to help the reader develop a range of spiritual disciplines. Feel free to include as much or as little of that in your meetings as you'd like. The details provided in How to Use This Study (pp. 11–13) will be helpful to you and all your group members, so be sure to review that information together!

It's up to you and your group how you'd like to structure your meetings, but we suggest including time for discussion of the week's study and Bible text, mutual encouragement, and prayer. You may also want to practice your Scripture memory verses together as a group or in pairs. As you share with each other, "consider how to stir up one another to love and good works" (Hebrews 10:24) and "encourage one another and build one another up" (1 Thessalonians 5:11).

Here are some sample questions to help facilitate discussion. This is structured as a weekly study, but if your group meets at a different frequency, you may wish to adjust the questions accordingly. Cover as many questions as time allows, or feel free to come up with your own. And don't forget to check out the additional resources we've linked for you at MyDGroup.org/Resources/John.

Sample Discussion Questions

What questions did this week's study or Bible text bring up for you?

What stood out to you in this week's study?

What did you notice about God and His character?

How were you challenged by your study of the Bible text? Is there anything you want to change in light of what you learned?

How does what you learned about God affect the way you live in community?

What correlation did you see between the psalm from Day 6 and this week's study of Jesus as God?

Have you felt God working in you through the weekly challenge? If so, how?

Is your love for God's Word increasing as we go through this study? If so, how?

Did anything you learned increase your joy in knowing Jesus?

ACKNOWLEDGMENTS

Olivia Le, who makes all our Writing Summits run smoothly—from flights to food to fun times!

Laura Buchelt, who built out a great structure for us and serves as our best encourager.

Emily Pickell, who is steady and unflappable, always bringing rich insights and wisdom.

Meg Mitchell, who finished out this study beautifully while also growing a human.

Meredith Knox, who provided awe-inducing content *and* comic relief.

Liz Suggs, who brought all her table-reading professionalism into the chaos of our new process.

Lisa Jackson, Jeff Braun, and Hannah Ahlfield, who cheer us on and keep us from stumbling as we move at this rapid pace.

ABOUT THE EDITOR

TARA-LEIGH COBBLE'S zeal for biblical literacy led her to create a network of Bible studies called D-Group (Discipleship Group). Every week, hundreds of men's and women's D-Groups meet in homes, in churches, and online for Bible study and accountability.

She also writes and hosts a daily podcast called *The Bible Recap* designed to help listeners read, understand, and love the Bible in a year. The podcast reached number one on the Apple Podcast Charts in All Categories and has garnered over four hundred million downloads, and more than twenty thousand churches around the world have joined their reading plan to know and love God better. It has been turned into a book published by Bethany House Publishers, with over five hundred thousand copies sold.

Tara-Leigh is a *Wall Street Journal* bestselling author, speaks to a wide variety of audiences, and regularly leads teaching trips to Israel because she loves to watch others be awed by the story of Scripture through firsthand experience.

Her favorite things include sparkling water and days that are 72 degrees with 55 percent humidity, and she thinks every meal tastes better when eaten outside. She lives in a concrete box in the skies of Dallas, Texas, where she has no pets, children, or anything that might die if she forgets to feed it.

For more information about Tara-Leigh and her ministries, you can visit her online.

Websites: taraleighcobble.com | thebiblerecap.com | mydgroup.org | israelux.com
Social media: @taraleighcobble | @thebiblerecap | @mydgroup | @israeluxtours